Get What You Want

Get Clear, Get Real & Get Going

Get What You Want

Get Clear, Get Real & Get Going

Lisa M. Zawistowski

Copyright © 2019 by Lisa M. Zawistowski

All rights reserved. No part of this book may be used or reproduced in any manner whatsoever including Internet usage, without the written permission of the author.

www.smallsteps2bigchange.com

Badass Books Publishing
www.badassbookspublishing.com

ISBN: 978-1-7347711-1-4
eBook ISBN: 978-1-7347711-0-7

Printed in the United States of America

Library of Congress Cataloging-in-Publication data is available upon request.

First paperback edition April 2020

For all those who champion my dreams…you know who you are…

I am always and forever grateful.

No one gets where she wants to go all on her own.

Contents

A Brief Introduction... ix

Prologue- The Official One, Like All Bona Fide And Stuff... xvii

PART I: GET CLEAR..1

Chapter 1: Know What Kind Of Eggs You Like 3

Chapter 2: Your Swot Team Has Your Back. Your S.w.o.t. Strengths, Weaknesses, Opportunities, Threats Analysis 12

Chapter 3: What's The Chatter? What The Voices In Your Head Are Saying About You. And The Accent Is Definitely Jersey........ 22

Chapter 4: The "Letting Go" Ceremony: How To Take Out The Trash For Rejection Hoarders.. 39

Chapter 5: Purpose: The 'P' Word You Can't Get Enough Of............... 48

Chapter 6: But What Do I Want? How To Find What You Want When All You Know Is That You Don't Have It Right Now 62

Chapter 7: Know Your Role Models. Also Known As, How Not To Reinvent The Wheel Because Oh, By The Way, Wheels Exist.. 73

PART II: GET REAL 87

Chapter 8: Regain Wonder. Seeing The World Through The Eyes Of A Child While Still Being Able To Drink Jack Daniels And Swear Like A Sailor 89

Chapter 9: Create A Bucket List.. 99

Chapter 10: Rewrite Your Story. Be Your Own Fucking Fairy
       Godmother And Buy Your Own Shoes And Dress 109

Chapter 11: From Vision Board To Ouija Board: Let
       The Magic Begin With Visual Cues 120

PART III: GET GOING 129

Chapter 12: Avoid The Frying Pan. Tuning In To Your
       Intuition Because You Hate Cast Iron 131

Chapter 13: Throw A Coming Out Party 145

Chapter 14: Regret Is A Motherfucker 153

Epilogue. And Shameless Plug For The Next Book Where
We Go Deeper. 161

My Bucket List 171

Resources: Aka. Stuff I Ridiculously Love So You Might Too 174

Author Bio: Lisa M. Zawistowski 177

Acknowledgements 178

A brief introduction

From there to here…because our stories all begin somewhere not of our choosing.

It was a balmy late spring night. The sun had just begun its descent. I stood in my usual spot with the others. Cars pulled through the dirt semicircle, and one by one, girls hopped in or out. Cars drove off, and girls in leotards, bags slung over their shoulders, chattered and bobbed down the stairs behind me.

The commotion quieted once again. The sky streaked with pink, shone enough light for the few robins looking for the last bits of the day's food in the grass nearby. I welcomed the silence. There was no need to worry about being good enough here. There was no front line-back line hierarchy in the yard the way there is in dance class. My thoughts could just rest on the robins, as I shifted in my outfit, distracted by the slightly scratchy texture and inky blackness of the leotard and tights. I longed for next year when I would be able to depart from the dancer-newbie uniform and choose colors. I already knew I wanted a royal blue leotard and ballet-pink tights. Lots of the other girls chose those colors. They looked like proper ballerinas. I wanted to look like them. That's what lots of girls did in the third year, wear those colors yet switch to the sheer coolness of jazz classes. It would be a welcome relief from the ennui of black-on-black attire and ballet-tap combo baby classes where everyone began.

Miss Audrey's School of Dance was the only dance school for twenty miles. Miss Audrey was a formidable woman. She was tall like my mom and always wore tights, a leotard, and a ballet skirt. Sometimes she still had her gold high-heeled tap shoes on from the class before. They were sparkly, and I liked them more than I liked Miss Audrey herself. The dance studio, in the basement of Miss Audrey's house, was comprised of a small waiting room decorated in the browns, oranges, and lime-green hues that permeated the 1970s. The studio was one room with a bathroom on the left side and three walls lined with mirrors and ballet barres. A door separated the two rooms as parents were not permitted to watch the classes. Every class started at the barre. Ballet first, then we got to change shoes and get to the good stuff.

As I stood there observing the fine details of the environment, the breeze blew the wisps of hair that never stayed in my ponytail, creating an exasperating tickle on my forehead. New sets of cars began to come in. Surely my mom is one of them. My eyes flashed to each car, looking for the sage-green Datsun. I didn't think too much about it, other than that I had to pee.

Picking me up on time wasn't exactly my mom's M.O. I spent a lot of time waiting for her or being hurriedly dressed and rushed out of the house. I once went to kindergarten wearing only a gold outerwear button-down sweater for a top because, well, she overslept. This was the kindergarten she bullied people to get me into because my birthday, September seventh, was actually a few days past the cutoff. She assured them I would be there and that she wasn't paying for another year of childcare because I didn't turn five until the end of the first week of school. (Note to self: Know what you want. Get what you want. Be polite but don't take no for an answer.)

The last group of girls that had bobbed down the stairs were now bobbing back up them and into cars as a new group exited cars and hurriedly shared all the news on the way down to class.

I contemplated rushing down the stairs and into the bathroom in the studio, but we weren't allowed back in once our class was over. Classes happened in rapid succession on Friday nights, and interrupting class was forbidden. Miss Audrey meant business when she reminded us of the rules at the beginning of each class. She was stern mostly, except that she was syrupy sweet to some of the girls and their mothers. Truth told, I really didn't want Miss Audrey to know that I hadn't been picked up yet. My mom and I didn't get the sugary version of her. Besides surely my mom was almost here. Most Friday nights my nana picked me up and she was always there waiting in car line when I got out.

My robins had flown off; the sky faded to black. The little porch light above the studio entry door was glowing a soft white. Streetlights across the street added iridescent spotlights to the asphalt. I was sick of my own thoughts, which had turned from reflection mixed with curiosity about the birds and sky to thoughts of my own discomfort- loneliness and fear *and* an overfull bladder. I felt taken over by the dismal yet familiar embarrassment of maybe having to make excuses for why my mom was late, like really late. And the truth is, I didn't know.

Standing there alone, and uncertain, I felt the wet, hot torrent as my bladder gave out and my shoes filled with urine. My mom wasn't going to be okay with this. I would need these washed for next Friday. Plus, she'd probably be able to tell as soon as I got in the car. Maybe if she didn't find out, I could wash them in the bathroom sink and set them to dry in my closet.

My mom was many things that started with "im" and "in"…impatient, intolerant, impossible, insensitive, immovable, and inconsistent. She'd dealt with a lot by age twenty: abusive father, baby, marriage, divorce, an unwanted change in career plans—none of it exactly her choosing. She kept her parents at an emotional arm's length, at the end of which she left an open hand dangling for my nana to put money into when my mother needed it. My mother's vitriol was not returned in kind, though it would have perhaps been justified.

As my mind plotted how to skirt trouble, my mom pulled in the driveway at top speed, practically sideways, as if that mattered now. It was way too late to try not to be late. And besides, I wouldn't bring it up. I was a six-year-old who peed her tights on the edge of a driveway outside a dance studio. That she was two hours late would take a backseat to shaming me.

"I fell asleep," she mumbled as I climbed into the car, my shaky hands fumbling at closing the door. We rode off in silence. Whether it was drugs or drowsiness, she didn't notice the smell of urine. I'd live to see another day.

Now as an adult and mother, I think about that scene and that child and know how I would have done nearly every part of it differently. I'd have gotten to know Miss Audrey a little so that my child felt slightly comfortable. I'd have been waiting in the car line to pick her up. I would have practiced dance steps with her and shown an interest in what she was learning. I would have asked her about the other girls and learned her friends' names. I would have done her hair in a bun because that's what she wanted. I would have thrown her the best ballet (or jazz)-themed birthday party ever and invited all her friends. I would have snuck something sparkly into her dance bag to make her feel special. We'd have picked up a pizza on the way home because I would know that she was hungry.

Fast forward twenty years. I learned to be the parent that I always wanted, first for my children and now for myself. I learned how to show up for myself. And I'm always right on time.

Who We Are…

Your story might start out a little different or a lot different, but we have arrived in the same place. Tired. Changed by life. Busy, but not ungrateful for what we have. Yet, somewhere in us is the flicker of all we ever dreamed about…a purpose. A destiny. We know the women we are meant to fully become. You know, that amazing woman that you are, which your friends remind you about via text messages while you're falling apart. They listen and then reassure you that you're tough as nails and compassionate as fuck and if we weren't us, we'd want to be us.

Yes, life is hard. And awesome. Challenging. Rewarding.

We are mothers, wives, coworkers, sisters, colleagues, entrepreneurs, friends, daughters, and teachers. We are leaders.

We are women meant for more.

"These gifts I give unto you. Greater work shall you do." This mantra has played in my head too many times to count since I was a little kid surviving. I assumed it was a Bible verse I'd heard at one of the Sunday school classes I attended with my nana…the ones that inspired my mother to label me a holy roller. I was aware early on that I didn't fit in with any organized religion that I knew of, because I understood that it was better to be a kind, compassionate person than anything else I could be. I had a relationship with God that wasn't fear or fire and brimstone. I could never be like the church ladies who didn't open their purse strings for people less fortunate than themselves even though they had the means. I couldn't be one of the ones who judged others before they even left God's house. I couldn't find those words in the Bible. Maybe they're in there or maybe they aren't. Either way, I know it's God talking to me. And, through me, to you.

You've come into this world endowed with gifts, a purpose and the ability to feel great passion. You were born knowing that you are Meant for More…

We are grateful for what we have while we work toward what we want.

If you are meant for more, you must do more…

Change your family's legacy.

Change the world.

Be the connector and leader of yourself, your family, business, community and maybe your country. Be the role model that is so needed. Change the world for kids, animals, our elders, the planet.

We can wear pearls or sequins. Drink bourbon or champagne. Swear like a sailor or don't. We are witty, fun, funny, serious, cerebral, soulful, carefree- except when we're worrying. We are full of love, scarred by pain, and we know the value of lifting others up.

A brief introduction

We are simple yet complicated.

We are all things. We were born all things and life is the journey back to being all things and being comfortable with it. Our lives are about reunification with what we repressed because we thought it wasn't good enough. It's about acceptance of who we are and standing unapologetically in the power of it.

You're already so many things. All amazing. But you are meant for more. You know it. You can get what you want. And you don't want or need to feel guilty about it. Step into it. I'm right here with you.

Why did I write this?

Someone recently asked me how I came to be so confident. Caught off guard, I said I've always been confident. That's not true at all. This book and the ones that follow it were written because even though I had been confident, or at least courageous, I found myself in a space where I was neither. I advocated fiercely for my kids' needs and secured as many of their wants as possible. But I wasn't advocating for my own and at last it trickled down to things that mattered to them. Thankfully, a spotlight shone on just how far away I was from that woman who'd gotten herself into college as a classical ballet major, then into business college, grad school and corporate jobs. The woman who, still a teenager, convinced her mother to bring her then-boyfriend to Florida for the summer because she wasn't leaving the best thing that'd ever happened to her behind in Erie, Pa. That woman was a boss. So, where did she go?

The lightbulb moment.

Every Friday night I went through the same McDonald's drive thru and I ordered the same chicken McNuggets happy meal with a chocolate milk. I did this for a couple years at least. It was the reward my young son with a learning disability got for working so hard at school. School was difficult for him, agonizing at times. The chicken nuggets and French fries were my way of saying, "Good job, you hard-worker, you." He looked forward to it all week.

On this particular night, my daughter Alexa, then twelve, was with me. I went through the drive-thru and ordered the food for my son. I got to the window, traded money for a bag of happiness and handed it to her. I asked her to check it. She looked in the odd container in there and said, "Mom, this isn't chicken nuggets." I had pulled ahead to the end of the drive-thru already. There was a hamburger patty thrown into a box and a small bag of fries. Somehow as my mind jumped ahead to solving this problem, I said, "That's okay. As long as the French fries are in there, I'll make him some chicken nuggets at home." My daughter looked at me like I had three heads.

"Mom. Pull around and go inside and get Jason's chicken nuggets that you paid for." I muttered about how I had some frozen ones in the freezer and I'd just heat those. "Mom, pull the car around into a spot and I'll go in and get his food."

I kowtowed with the keen sense that she was not going to give up. I did what she said and not five minutes later she pops back out to the car with chicken nuggets, fresh French fries and an ice cream cone for herself, a free gift for her troubles. I can only imagine what she was thinking. It was very clear to her how this needed to be handled and she was right. I, on the other hand, was willing to make my son sacrifice part of his reward for not-as-good frozen chicken nuggets that he'd have to wait for and I'd have to do work to prepare, when I had paid for someone else to give me what we all really wanted.

I drove away metaphorically scratching my head. And I understood that I needed to regroup. How did I get here? What else was I settling for? Thankfully, when a twelve-year-old handed me a lesson in a McDonald's drive-thru, I paid attention. It was the get what you want lesson. I realized that if I could get to this place of diminished confidence, for whatever reason, other women might be experiencing this too. Our journal entries may look different, but the path out is the same. Be polite but get what you want.

Confidence is a skill, not a trait. You don't get it from your DNA. You don't have to ever have had confidence to gain confidence. You just must want it and be willing to do the work. You have what it takes because you are a woman meant for more. Learn. Unleash. You 2.0. #womenmeantformore #getwhatyouwant

Prologue- the official one, like all bona fide and stuff...

What does "get what you want" mean, exactly? I will explain this because you don't know me. You don't know that I am a relentless compassionista and that I would never ever intentionally do anything unkind to anyone or anything even though I occasionally sound like that girl from the streets of Jersey. If I sound like a wise guy or a scrapper, it is for humor's sake, drawing on my roots. I like to make people laugh. My life has given me much material.

What "get what you want" *is not*:
Ruthless and abrasive. Egotistical. Selfish. Cheeky. Neither is it even remotely narcissistic (you know, that characteristic we all feel we're becoming when we focus on ourselves for even a minute).

When you pause for a moment, you realize the better question is why the hell not get what you want so you can be even more fabulous and do bigger and better things for yourself and others? I mean, nobody gets what she wants *all* the time. But those of us with a "get what you want" mindset, get what we want way more often than those without one. We get what we want more than someone with an "I'll take what comes" mindset. We get what we want more than the person who thinks "this is as good as it gets" or "it is what it is." The bottom line is that you get what you focus on so you want to figure out for sure what will make you the lasting kind of happy and focus on that like your life depends on it.

To that end, I explain, in the very first chapter of this book, how to get clear about what you really do want and what makes you happy. You create your life with your thoughts, emotions, and actions. You want a rich life that you *ridiculously* love, not just a life you like, tolerate, or put up with. You want more than to simply check boxes or meet your most basic needs. You want to do more than power through.

You want to get unstuck.

When you **Get Clear** about what you want, that which is aligned with your life's purpose, the Universe conspires to help you get it.

Seems easy enough, right?

Here's the complicated part. Most people are naturally better at articulating what they don't want to be, do, or have in their lives. You get what you focus on, so thinking about what you don't want actually creates more of that.

Getting clear involves creating a specific list with vivid details about what you want.

Simple example…You don't want the big U (Universe) to help you get a Gucci bag when you're really melty in the knees for a Louis Vuitton. You don't want the U to think you want to become a clinical psychologist when you really want to be a life coach. You can't be vague on the details.

What do you want?

I had a client, Kate, who, after many life challenges including being homeless for a year with her young son, said she just wanted to be comfortable. But what does that mean? I said to her, "Kate, you've got to be more specific than that or the Universe is going to send you sweatpants." Be specific. Like, really specific. Say exactly what you want and don't feel guilty about it. And don't play small or you'll get small.

Unleash. What does You 2.0 want?

Getting clear is just the beginning, however. We must also **Get Real** about where we are versus where we want to be and what has to change. Here we will dig deep and be honest with ourselves. We will commit to the changes we must make and consummate our vow with the first small steps. I mean, if you didn't need to change anything, you'd already be who you want to become, have what you heart desires, and be living a life you crazy love. But you're not. Yet.

After we get real, we immediately **Get Going**. There is power in small steps. Big leaps are great too. But the energy of a single small step beckons the next and the one after that.

Get Clear + Get Real + Get Going = Get What You Want

It's simple addition and reliable the way math always is. 2+2=4 and getting clear, getting real and getting going gives you what you want. Don't be frightened off by the math analogy. Even if you're not good at math or with numbers, you can do addition. And you can get what you want. I promise. If you do the work, you get what you want.

Why does it work?

The mechanisms of human motivation and change are the same no matter whether you want to lose weight, start your own business, find the love of your life, have more meaningful friendships, be more successful in your career, find your dream job, and become the best version of you.

I wasn't always living a life I loved. I had the great guy and amazing kiddos, but I was still completely drained by not having a career I ridiculously loved. I not only gave myself permission to find it, do it and become the best version of myself but I also gave myself a kick in the ass right on out of my comfort zone. The universe gave me one too, and I decided it was time.

I can help you get there too.

The practical stuff about me.

I've studied business and psychology at the undergraduate and graduate level. I've dabbled in positive psychology. I'm a certified strategic intervention coach through Anthony Robbins' training program. Mostly, I've done a bit of what I didn't love along the way to figuring out what I do love. Nothing is wasted. Finding our authentic selves, our soul's mission and the delicious life is always right on divine time. You're not too late or behind the ball. When you're ready, the teacher appears. You'll feel the vibration and know you're seeing something that's meant for you. A puzzle piece. If you pay attention, the opportunities follow, sometimes with lightning speed and sometimes a bit slower but they always come.

I'm a Jersey girl with a kind heart and a big dream to help you be happier.

Fulfilling your purpose feels euphoric. Living a life you love with people who lift you up and light you up, and work that sets your soul on fire is the best feeling ever. You feel aligned. You're excited to get out of bed every day and happy to come home from vacation. It's a spiritual experience like when you meet the love of your life and when hold your baby for the first time. This is why I must share what I have learned, the book learning and what life has shown me, with you. You want all that fans your inner flame! All of it! The full Monty of life's awesomeness. And you shall have it.

You are meant for more.

God, The Universe, the Goddess wants you to be, have and do all that makes an amazing life for you. You have a purpose and you feel passion when you find it. Just like love made the Velveteen Rabbit real, you living your best life makes you real. Yes, to all of it.

Be who you're meant to be.

Do what you're meant to do.

Have what your heart desires.

Say yes.

Life is short…or maybe it's long…it doesn't matter if you aren't living a life you ridiculously love!

If you aren't smiling so often people wonder what you're up to…things need to change. If you're still breathing, it's not too late. Regret is a motherfucker.

Walk with me…let's create a life you crazy love. Not merely like. Not "don't hate it". Ridiculously fucking love. I know for sure that you're worth it.

Love and hugs,
Lisa Z.

P.S. As you can tell there is a wee bit of swearing in this book. It is not gratuitously done but if you were hanging out with me, having laughs and cocktails whilst talking about life, there'd be swearing, particularly the F word. I'm candid and honest. Everything here is to the best of my recollection. I do not strive for perfection. I love you and I sincerely want you to be happy. That is the reason I am willing to venture into the realm of much better writers, more educated psychologists and those who would otherwise criticize my work. Things that are repeated are (mostly) intended to be so they stick. I've a long-standing love affair with Merriam Webster. I refer to her as my gal pal Merriam in a lot of my work. I don't have a large vocabulary and I was not educated as a writer, so I rely on her. I do love words so much. They can transcend boundaries, time and space. And they can change lives.

I'm in the arena so I can lead you to become the woman who bravely and confidently creates a life she ridiculously loves. I am right here with you. And for you.

#womenmeantformore
#getwhatyouwant

PART I
GET CLEAR

WE MUST BEGIN AT THE BEGINNING

"Everyone who got where he is had to begin where he was."
-Robert Louis Stevenson

CHAPTER 1

Know What Kind of Eggs You Like

"You're so lost, you don't even know what kind of eggs you like!"
-Ike Graham,

A character played by Richard Gere in the movie Runaway Bride ... because everything we need to know about life can be found in a Julia Roberts movie. Right?

In the movie, Runaway Bride with Richard Gere and Julia Roberts, Gere's character, a journalist documenting the antics of the bride who runs away from the altar, realizes that Robert's character becomes whoever the person she's about to marry needs her to be, including eating whatever kind of eggs he likes for breakfast. At the turning point of the film, Gere says to her, "What kind of eggs do *you* like?" She didn't know the answer. She didn't know herself as an individual, independent of whomever she was in a relationship with. Though the movie is about a fictional character, we can lose our identity for many reasons: needing to please or seeking the approval of others, never bothering to figure out who we are, over identifying with one or more of our roles (CEO, mom, daughter, caregiver) or simply because we aren't secure in our own skin. The point where we lie awake in bed in the middle of the night, disquieted by the realization that we don't know what we want or even who we are anymore, can happen at any time but often coincides with entering a new phase in our lives, such as after the kids leave home, or following a divorce, the loss of a loved one, or the end of a significant career position. Not knowing what we want also happens as a result of feeling stuck and hopeless, feeling that your situation can't change because you don't know how to change it.

Though I love a good shortcut as much as the next guy, we must begin at the beginning. The beginning is to articulate exactly what you love, like, tolerate, dislike, and what the complete fucking deal breakers are that you are not going to have in your life in this new phase (even if they're in your life now). YOU. Meet YOU. Get to know yourself like you're on a first date. One you're excited about. Not the one with the nice boy your mom keeps trying (relentlessly) to set you up with.

A happy life is loaded with loves and likes, has as few things as possible that you tolerate and dislike, and includes NO deal breakers.

You, gorgeous nurturer to all, undoubtedly put up with a ton of shit that isn't good for you and isn't in sync with your values, passions, or happiness but you're too nice to get rid of it, just like you're too nice (restrained) to say the F word (as often as you'd like to). That's okay. I'm here now. I'll help you sort it out. And I will be standing behind you as you let go of things you don't like and whilst you kick the deal breakers right out the front door before slamming it shut and changing the locks.

Note: For all the exercises in this book you can write in your journal, if you have one, and if you're not a journaler, a simple notebook will do nicely. Fancy schmancy is not necessary but the work is.

Glittery or plain Jane is up to you. Get what you want. You will read that phrase 367 more times before you get to the last page of this book. Rehearsal maintenance. Read it until you believe it. When you believe it, it becomes a way of life.

It's important to write out all the answers for the exercises so that you can reflect on them, and if you're no longer twenty-something, so you can remember them. Visual prompts and introspection. Particularly when our minds are wrought with frustration, like the kind that might come from precious time lost in work, relationships or a version of yourself you don't love, it's difficult to unjumble our thoughts, feelings and beliefs. But it's necessary that we do just that. Writing your responses to the work I ask you to do is the great facilitator.

The Know What Kind of Eggs You Like Exercise.
Time to make your lists.

Directions:
1. Make five columns side by side on a page.
2. At the top of each column, place your labels: **Loves, Likes, Tolerations, Dislikes, and Deal Breakers.**
3. Make lists of things you love, like, merely tolerate, dislike, and things that you really despise.

Let the lists be long and flowy like an oversized floral print mu-mu. Get to know yourself. Write down the weird, whacky, and wild things alongside the mundane stuff, like a love of pancakes and syrup. Include foods, colors, sounds, places, characteristics, feelings, personality traits, and tasks. If lying is a pet-peeve of yours, put it in the Deal Breakers column. Record the good, bad, ugly, and so-so.

What you write down can be things that are currently in your life, or not in your life yet, but you want them to be (Loves & Likes). Let your brain go wild. Let it fantasize. Don't qualify, quantify, classify, criticize, or in any way judge your answers. Yes, I know it's tough. You want to come up with all the right answers and get an A. Well there's no A, overachiever, only truth. Just write down what comes to mind. Go back and add to the lists later if you think of things you missed. Things I've learned: a glass of wine or two helps the truth rise to the top. No need to be proper or in control here. Let loose. Doing this exercise fully is like achieving orgasm, if you're too uptight, it won't happen. And like masturbation, this exercise isn't for, against, or even remotely about anyone else but you. Get used to focusing on you. Don't feel guilty. Don't apologize. And, no, you're not becoming a narcissist. Believe me, when you're happily the best version of you, everyone else wins. Except your enemies. They lose and die. Okay, not die. But definitely lose.

I really want you to be free and not focused on any constraints, but this is our first exercise together so I'm going to share some examples to get you going…

Here's what your lists might look like:

Love: helping others (duh!), reading, being outside in nature, working with numbers, solving problems, spending time with family, dogs, cats, turtles, being around animals, cooking, doing random acts of kindness, showing compassion, hugs, traveling, writing, happy people, eating delicious food, chocolate, getting enough sleep, coffee, learning new things, salsa dancing, just salsa (no dancing)

Like: spending time with friends, going to church, yoga, volunteering, gardening, painting, watching comedies, shopping, reading fashion magazines, martinis, being by the water, going to the beach, working three hours a day but making more money than you did when you worked 10 hours a day

Tolerate: getting up early, cleaning the house, homework, exercising, learning the technical aspects of having an online business, paying bills, talking on the phone, coloring your roots every three weeks, spending time with "those" family members (you know the ones)

Dislike: narcissists, dishonesty, cruelty of any kind, working at a job you don't love (but happen to be good at), spending time with people that drain your energy, saying yes when you really mean no, saying no when you really mean yes (because you don't think you have enough time, energy or money), not having more free time, five hours of sleep, that dust keeps coming back and multiplying, that your dog is happier than you

Deal breakers: lying, maliciousness, negativity, being stuck in the past, extreme levels of narcissism, lack of empathy, excessive takers, halitosis, superficiality, racism, sexism, anything immoral, unethical, or unkind, judgment, disloyalty, cheating, doing gymnastics while intoxicated (because you like your neck in good working order)

When you look at your lists, do you have more *likes* and *loves* or more *tolerates* and *dislikes*?

The perspective problem.

If you have more tolerates and dislikes, part of the problem may lie in your perspective.

You may be more in touch with what you don't like and not focused enough on what you do like. Negative perspective is learned behavior and culturally reinforced in the American culture. If you tend to think about what's wrong and what you don't have (rather than what's right and what you do have) someone in your early environment probably taught you to think like that. You can unlearn it.

You choose what you focus on.

And what you focus on you see, get, and bring more of into your life. Law of Attraction, Lovely. If you decide you're going to go out today and see yellow butterflies, you will find yellow butterflies or at least a picture of them.

Let yourself go.

Step away from the world as you know it.

Really tune in to what makes you smile, feel joy, and feel the flutter of excitement in your heart. Put those things in your Loves and Likes columns.

Bye bye crapola.

If you thought it was tough to focus on what you want more of, hold onto your hat because now we're going to get you face to face with the giant load of shit you accept, settle for, power through, make excuses about, and deal with because you didn't realize you have the power to change it. It really doesn't matter why you developed this tendency to tolerate, or that it's reinforced by the female stereotype, what matters is that you can change it. You can decide, right now, that you are going to be less tolerant. That's not the same as less compassionate or less understanding. Less compassionate would be bitchy and unkind. Less tolerant is you getting rid of stuff you don't want anyway.

You may be putting up with some things that are deal breakers for you because you're more uncomfortable with change than you are with your current situation. But putting up with deal breakers festers below the surface like toxic sludge that slowly makes you sick. You can't be completely happy living with things you secretly hate or while swimming in tolerations and dislikes.

Warning: You may be lying to yourself about whether things are deal breakers, saying they aren't when they are, having gradually numbed your brain and heart into believing, willing accomplices.

Do you find yourself saying things like: it's not that bad (about your soul sucking job, friends, partner, in laws), he has more good qualities than bad ones, you get used to it, no job (man, house, life) is perfect. If you're saying anything like these sentences, you've settled. They might be true, but they also indicate that you're making do. You're not happy but you don't know how to (or think you can't) change it to something better.

You make excuses about why you're putting up with it because you're not ready to deal with it. Maybe you still think it'll get better. You may be saying something in your life, work, or relationships isn't a deal breaker for you, when really it is, just so you don't have to justify, even to yourself, why you're not doing anything about it. I've done this too. I've stayed in jobs way past when it was good for me, past the point that I was happy and long after there was any further opportunity for me. Your soul, the untrickable essence of you, always knows better.

Here's my opinion about unhappiness.

If you're not happy with your job, yourself, your relationships, or your life, change something immediately.

Rock your boat.

You're reading this book because you want to make your happiness a priority. Sometimes, we settle for being happy in one area, but not in others, and it's almost like you don't want to rock the boat if even one part of your life is going swimmingly well. I'm here to tell you to go for all of it! What's the worst that can happen? You end up with a life you ridiculously love? That's the big goal. It's what God intended for you. It's why happy feels good and crappy doesn't; it's a guidance system.

Pile your life high, like an oversized New York deli sandwich, with what you love and like. Tip the scale in favor of everyday joy. The side that has loves and likes must outweigh the side that has tolerations and dislikes. At the risk of sounding like a broken record, no deal breakers. If the tolerations and dislikes side is heavier, take one thing off. And then another. You won't be able to remove all the tolerations and dislikes from your life as we all must pay taxes, drive in traffic, and clean the toilet from time to time, but pile on the likes and loves to compensate for what you must do but don't want to.

If you can't identify at least ten loves and ten likes, spend some time in the relationship with yourself. You, for sure, know what you don't love, don't like and don't want. You can't focus on that or you'll attract more of it. There can only be Mr. or Ms. Wrongs if you don't know who you are right now. When you aren't clear about who you are and what you love, you will do what you always did and continue to get the same things that haven't made you completely happy or fulfilled. Start with finding answers to simple questions like what would you read if you were on a vacation by yourself and not reading about weight-loss, self-improvement, or career related stuff? What would you read by the pool while the smoking hot cabana guy brings you fruity drinks with tropical flowers in them? What kind of restaurant would you go to, and what would you wear if you were on a date with yourself? What's your favorite color? Flower? Perfume?

And yes, know what kind of eggs you like. Or acknowledge that you fucking hate eggs and everything else that comes out the back end of a chicken.

NOTES

The journey of a thousand miles begins with knowing what you love and like.

What I *ridiculously* love in this chapter:

I will make my lists of Loves, Likes, Tolerations, Dislikes and Deal-breakers by (insert date):

One thing I love is:

Affirmation:

I know myself better and prioritize my happiness.

CHAPTER 2

Your SWOT team has your back. Your S.W.O.T. Strengths, Weaknesses, Opportunities, Threats Analysis

The world is all gates, all opportunities, strings of tension waiting to be struck.
-Ralph Waldo Emerson,
Poet, essayist, philosopher

A SWOT analysis is a tool used in business strategic planning. It's an assessment of strengths, weaknesses, opportunities and threats regarding a business idea, a new venture, new product, or existing products. When I performed SWOT analyses as a marketing manager, I wrote everything that came to mind about the market, it's products distribution, customer wants and competitive threats into one of these four categories. Then I considered more carefully what I knew about my market, what I knew about similar and different markets the company served and added to what I had brainstormed. I shared the data with other marketing managers to see if anyone could think of things I might be missing. When you're using this tool in business planning, there's no emotion and your job is to be as thorough and honest as possible. The well-being of the company, and certainly your part of it, rides on your accuracy.

> *Life is a business; we are all entrepreneurs.*

Your happy life is your business. We are all entrepreneurs in that respect. The creation of a joyful life requires excavation, skill, thought, a plan and action. From time to time, you analyze what's working and what's not and make changes. We, usually, feel more emotional about our lives than our work, but not necessarily the corresponding work ethic to fix what isn't working. Therein lies the problem. We get mired in the emotion of what's shown up and stop short of fixing what needs fixing. You may be more determined to do a good job at work than you are at life. There you have peer pressure, yearly evaluations and you could get fired if you don't meet expectations. You might have intrinsic motivation to do well at work but you for sure have extrinsic reasons to do well. We are often proactive and tenacious creators at work, yet passive and reactive in our life strategies. But how great would life be if you use the same analytical skills and problem solving you employ at work in your life. Do more of what you're good at and less of what you're not. Your SWOT team has your back. Excavation part two.

SWOT Exercise.

Take a piece of paper and draw a horizontal line dividing the paper in half and then a vertical line dividing it in half lengthwise. Label your quadrants Strengths, Weaknesses, Opportunities and Threats. As with the Loves, Likes exercise in chapter one, don't qualify, criticize or judge your answers. Give some thought about what should go into each of the quadrants. I will elaborate on each category and how it translates from corporate strategic planning to life, love and finding work that sets your soul on fire.

Strengths.

When you identify your strengths make sure you capture what you feel are your absolute best qualities, skills, and talents. What do you like most about yourself? What are you naturally good at? What do your friends, family, bosses and coworkers value about you? What's your thing that everyone knows you're excellent at doing? Are you detail-oriented, organized, a great listener, compassionate, able to meet deadlines, caring, master multitasker, patient? Strengths can include things like: overcomes adversity like a champ, is resilient, sees the positive in everything, hopeful, creative and helpful. Strengths can also be practical such as good with numbers, has analytical skills, stellar communication skills, is relatable. Strengths help you identify work you are most suited for and help you explain why you don't love your current job (doesn't utilize what you're naturally good at and doesn't embody what you like and love) even though you're good at it. I have a personal motto, "never let it be said that I did a shitty job at anything." What that does is make me determined to be good at anything I take on whether it's my work or being a great room mom on a field trip at my kid's school. I was a good student in school. However, being good at something doesn't mean you will be happy doing it. I was a good student in both undergraduate and graduate school for business. I had a few classes that I was really interested in, but mostly I looked at those degrees as a means to earn a decent living. I didn't know then that I would need much more than that. I hadn't looked at all of my strengths and chosen the ones are more important to me and my happiness. My practical brain was driving the car. My soul didn't find its voice until I had spent the tuition money and gotten my first job.

That said, no knowledge is ever wasted. You get the life experiences you are meant to have so you can become the person you are meant to be. No accidents and no coincidences. I might have had the opportunity to realize my love for psychology there and switched majors. I was in a college that has a very good school for psychology. Why couldn't fate have put me on that path- had me meet someone in the psychology program at a party and had them tell me things that would have peaked my curiosity or some other miraculous cause for awakening. The answer is because it was not meant to be. Studying business and finance was part of the plan of me becoming who I am meant to be. An expensive part. But also a valuable part.

So, after you write down all your strengths and no number is too many or too few (that would be a judgment), look at them. Which ones make you smile? Which ones resonate with you? Which ones speak to you above the others? Circle them. These are clues.

To use myself as an example, some of my strengths are as follows:

Good with numbers, practical, creative, compassionate, positive, optimistic, analytical, deadline driven, tenacious, adaptable

But out of those, positive, optimistic and compassionate are my favorite strengths. They feel different to me when I read those words compared to when my eyes roll over "deadline driven" or "analytical" even though they're all very true of me and all what I would consider my natural abilities.

Weaknesses.

Thankfully, we don't need to be good at everything. Everyone has weaknesses. Weaknesses are useful! They still show us bits of who we are in an important way. Weaknesses show us what we are not meant to be, do or emphasize. Weaknesses are traits you want to either build up so they become more like strengths or outsource. Spend your time doing work and activities that require few of your weaknesses and lots of your strengths. As an entrepreneur, I hire someone who can do those things (I'm not good at) better, faster and with less frustration. Spend more time on what you're best at. Efficiency model. This is true in your romantic relationships as well. Couples, especially parents, should explore each other's SWOT analysis. You are looking for complementary skills. If you are good with numbers and organization, you do the bills and budget. If you are lousy at money and it stresses you out but you're good with power tools, you get to fix stuff and your partner is hopefully good with money. If neither of you are good at a task, outsource. Have the conversations and find agreement based on natural abilities, education and preferences rather than on traditional roles for men and women or what worked for your or his parents and others you know. Solidarity is based on communication and complementary skills. No kidding. That bit of knowledge can save you a lot of time and aggravation. My husband doesn't remember numbers and I do, so I keep track of all important dates and anything else numbery. Rather than get mad because I have to tell him the exact date of the kids' birthdays, I understand that's a complementary skill. In return, he makes sure I never get lost when we travel anywhere. More times than not, I leave a store in the mall and walk in the direction I just came from instead of where I want to go. If it weren't for my husband being able to get us back to our hotel from anywhere, I'd still be wandering around Europe from our trip in 2007. Not a bad thing, but the kids needed to get back home for school. You and your mate will have a lot fewer disagreements if you understand each other's strengths and weaknesses and acknowledge that you both have them…which of course you do.

List your weaknesses and be honest about them. No judgment or criticism. We all have weaknesses. A weakness may be that you're an excessive giver of time or money. It may be that you are codependent. Maybe you're great at starting projects but not so great at finishing them. Maybe you aren't the most organized person. Maybe you aren't as detail-oriented as you want to be. Can't be on time if your life depends on it. Weakness are not qualities you want to change completely but they are qualities that would serve you well if you made them stronger or hired them out where possible. For me, I'm not good at technical stuff like programming the DVR or building my own website and adding plug-ins (whatever those are) so it works better. I have a husband and two kids that I rely on to handle the technical stuff around the house and I have a technical virtual assistant and web designer who handles all the technical work I need for my business.

It takes a village.

Opportunities.

While strengths and weaknesses are more self-explanatory, opportunities and threats, as they pertain to your life and relationships, need some explanation. Opportunities are chances for you to change things for the better. This could be losing weight, switching from underearner to sugar momma, getting your needs met in ways that are good for you, quitting smoking, eating healthier, creating more free time, becoming more organized, changing your credit score or financial situation, starting a three times a week yoga practice, getting eight hours of sleep, being able to set healthy boundaries- saying yes when you mean it and no when you mean no, starting that novel you've always wanted to write, going back to school, becoming more mindful and anything else you feel will create a higher level of well-being and happier life.

Opportunities are the possibilities in your environment that you have not seized. And maybe one of your opportunities is to build an opportunity mindset so that you can see them. You want to become an entrepreneur. You want to lose weight, so you feel healthier. You want to trade procrastination for success habits, before you face regret. You want to stop living in the past and write a new story for yourself. You want to stop dwelling on what you don't have and become as mentally and emotionally fit as possible, so you can have what you really want in life, love and career. You want to stop tolerating your current level of happiness and go for sparkly. There may be a person you have identified as a mentor but not reached out to them or read more about them to learn how they got where they are. There may be projects or volunteer work you've passed up that may be just the connections you need for some reason. You may have talked yourself out of applying for this job you'd love because you don't have all the requirements perfectly. You haven't put the energy out there to attract Mr. or Ms. Right. You've been in the comfort zone.

Don't be so worried about whether it's a mistake or you're not good enough.

There are no mistakes. ALL KNOWLEDGE IS VALUABLE. The word mistake is a label *you* give your actions and decisions. Very seldom does someone tell you that you made a mistake. Most often mistake is a label we use to classify our decisions and actions after the fact. You could just as easily call them something else. Learning experiences is the cliché term. You could make up your own name for experiences that taught you what not to do or what you don't want. Part of being certain about what you do want can only come from experience with what you don't want.

When you begin to think about opportunities, you'll see more of them. You get what you focus on. You can focus on what you lack or you can focus on what you want.

List all your opportunities- things you can achieve more easily and the bigger things you want but may take longer to achieve. Don't qualify your opportunities by whether you think it's possible. Whatever you want is possible. Opportunities are the small steps you can take today and tomorrow to move you forward to happiness.

Threats.

Threats are the saboteurs in your environment that are going to try to cock block the changes you want to make and oppose the new you you're trying to create. These may be family and friends who are more comfortable with you staying right where you are than moving in a shiny, positive direction. There will be pessimists and dream killers who will tell you they're just being realistic as they bring you down. Parents may tell you they're afraid for you or don't want you to be disappointed. Most people fail at long-term change. Most fall far short of creating a plan and sticking to it for more than a month. It may be easier, for the people closest to you, to identify with your problems than with your success and happiness. They may be programmed for crisis and be right there when a big problem arises but seem to not even pay attention when you're talking about the good things. They may be miserable and want to stay that way and want you to stay there too.

There will be energy vampires and naysayers in your environment that will need to go away or you will need to dramatically limit your time with them and feel good about doing it.

Write your threats. These can be things like: telling your mom your switching careers even though you know she won't approve, finding the money and time for the classes you need to re-educate yourself in your new direction, your own pessimistic mindset, your love of your comfort zone, fear of failure, fear of success, not knowing where to start, no support system, and negative self-talk. You might be your own worst enemy and it's not your fault. In the next chapter we will talk about the self-sabotage that comes from a lifetime of negative self-talk habits.

> *"Surround yourself only with people who are going to take you higher."*
> *-Oprah Winfrey*

Threats, as I mentioned, are the obstacles, barriers, naysayers, doubters and haters you will face as you commit to making changes and move in a new direction. Many, most or all of these doubters will be in your own head. You are going to have to become resolute in your decision to change. Everyone faces obstacles, feels overwhelmed from time to time and doubts they can get to the finish line. Even when you become clear about what you want and are making progress taking the steps to get there, you will have days where you will want to quit. Don't quit. Switch tasks, take a walk, hit the gym, meditate, hug your dog, read something inspiring, or whatever makes you feel better, without sabotaging your progress, but DO NOT QUIT. The only person who never reaches her goal is the one who gives up on it along the way. You are worthy of having what you want. And if you are still reading this, you must have a glimmer of belief that it's possible for you. You must get gritty not quitty.

> *"Too many people over value what they are not and under value what they are."*
> *-Malcolm Forbes*

Get excited about your strengths and opportunities. Your life will become easier and more meaningful as you become more aware of your natural abilities and align with those. When you make up your mind that the world is full of opportunities just waiting for you to seize them, that's exactly what you'll find. Pinky promise. Then, decide how you will deal with your weaknesses and combat the threats one small step at a time. This may require big girl britches and some hardcore honesty, but you've got this. You're a warrior.

Knowledge is power. Keep it simple.

Weakness = Strengthen or outsource
Threats= Evaluate and Tackle
Strengths + opportunities = Bountiful life

Great job, YOU! Now let's talk about those voices in your head.

NOTES

No one is given weaknesses without being given strengths.

What I ridiculously love in this chapter:

What I am naturally good at?

I will do my complete SWOT Analysis by (insert date):

Affirmation:

I will honor the natural abilities I have been given and use them as clues to fulfill my happiness and destiny.

CHAPTER 3

What's the Chatter? What the Voices in Your Head Are Saying About You. And the Accent Is Definitely Jersey.

(Except when it's Queens, Brooklyn, the Bronx, or Milwaukee, Wisconsin. The voices. You get the idea. You've heard them so many times.)

Mom: Ok. skin doctor/butcher appt today. Going to have an ugly spot on my leg cut off. Do u want to come with me to see the doctor?
Kate: Why on earth would I want to do that?
Mom: He's jewish and ur ovaries are rotting.
-Kate Friedman-Siegel,
@crazyjewishmom on Instagram

What the voices say.
"That'll never work."
"That's not practical."
"That's the stupidest idea I've ever heard."
"You don't have the commonsense God gave a grapefruit?" (Clever, right?)
"Be seen, not heard."
"Shush."
"I'm not worthy."
"I'm not good enough."

"I can't."
"I can't right now. Now's not the time."
"I don't know how."
"I'm not that lucky."
"Stuff works out for other people but not for me."
"I don't have what it takes."
"I'm a quitter."
Do any of these sound familiar?
Here are some other shit sandwiches I hear frequently:
"I'm too old, too fat, too busy, too tired, too blah, blah, blah."
"I'm not pretty enough."
"I've already chosen a path and I can't change it now."
How about:
"I don't have time." "I don't have the money." "I don't have the energy."

Some would say these are excuses. They would be right.

Unless, they were hardwired in your brain, overtly or subliminally, by someone you looked up to. Someone whose approval you sought. This is the difference between an excuse and a belief. Excuses are made by consenting adults and children who are not sufficiently motivated to do something.

Mom: Clean your room.

Kid: I can't right now; I'm watching the grass grow.

Mom: You need to get some groceries in your apartment so you can stop spending so much on takeout and cook some healthy food like a normal person.

Adult child: I can't right now; I'm binge watching all 200 seasons of Grey's Anatomy for the twelfth time.

Those are excuses.

You're thinking that you should apply for a new job to replace the one you currently have with a narcissist prick of a boss, stab-you-in-the-back coworkers, impossible deadlines on your real work because of the sheer number of unnecessary meetings scheduled by said boss and a salary that makes sure you never ever get ahead. Yet you can't find your resume to apply for new jobs and you don't think you have the qualifications to get a better job. Also, you haven't looked with more than a glance but you're sure there aren't any jobs out there for you unless you brush up on your skills and you don't have time to take a class. Those are your excuses. In this case they are the externalization of your internal beliefs. I'm not good enough. I don't have what it takes to get what I want. I can't do it because I'm not enough. Everyone else is better than me.

You can get over the excuses and when you're ready, you will.

When you get more uncomfortable where you are than with the idea of doing what you must do get somewhere new, you'll move.

Changing your core beliefs about yourself is a bit trickier. It could come down to a tipping point where you're sick to death of how your life is going. More likely, when the time is right, you hear someone say something and you feel like you just looked through a window into your soul. The message resonates with you. You dig deeper. You read. You listen. You learn. And slowly but surely you begin to challenge your beliefs.

But how do you begin?

I want to tell you something here, human to human, inner child to inner child. If you only do the work in one chapter in this whole book, do this one. If ever there is a short cut to a happier life, this is it. You don't have to set goals. You don't have to make your dreams come true. You don't have to meditate or grow your optimism. I highly recommend doing those things but if you only work the material in one chapter in this entire book or any other book for that matter, do this one. If you maintain your commitment to this work right here, you will be happier. You have negative messages in your head. The only variation among us is how many negative messages we have on repeat. How often per day you talk shit about yourself and how much does it sabotage your happiness and success?

Oh, the noise, noise, noise.

We have, on average, 80,000 mini conversations with ourselves every single day.

WTF? I know. How do we ever get anything done? Or get any peace. I was shocked by that number even though I'm acutely aware that my brain never stops yammering.

It has been estimated that 80% of these little orations (on average) are negative.

Think about that for a hot minute.

There is no way in hell that you can hear 64,000 derogatory remarks about yourself per day, or a whopping 23,360,000 in a year, and feel great about yourself! Multiply 23.4 million by your age, and you get the full weight of why you can't get where you want to go. Holy cannoli!

And even if you're not from Jersey, you wouldn't put up with anyone else talking shit about you like that. But you do it easily and effortlessly to yourself. It's the thing you're relentless about. That you suck. That you can't…because you're not enough. Any message, reinforced, sticks. Especially if you believe it's from a credible source, and you would consider yourself a credible source on how much you are just not fucking good enough. I mean, surely everyone else can see it too.

It's exhausting. How do we ever get out of bed?

Even if you only beat yourself up 50% of the time, that's still 40,000 messages a day.

Exactly how much are your beliefs working to your detriment and sadness? To your feelings of hopelessness? To the limits you place on who you can become, what you can do and have? How much are these powerful negative words shitting on your dreams?

No wonder we care so much about what everyone else thinks of us. We're looking for hope that we're wrong about ourselves. We're looking for validation that we're actually not that bad.

Every day you power through this negative self-talk and make the best of things. You try to live a good life. But how much happier could you be if you forbid yourself to talk shit about you? This includes your self-deprecating humor and the deflection of compliments given you. No more self-sabotage. Only good things. Dare I say it, the truth. The truth about you. And it's really good.

Imagine. (Cue the dream sequence music)

How would it feel if you only held positive thoughts about yourself? How would it be if your mind became a place of honor and peace for you and about you? How would it feel if you thought, "I've got this!" instead of I can't, I'm not good enough, or plain old, "I suck"? How would it feel if you could look in the mirror and see your own beauty because your beliefs now allowed you to see it? How would it feel to love what you see and hear from yourself? I'm here to tell you it's possible. I did it. I did not get there overnight, but I no longer hold any thoughts other than loving and supportive ones for myself. I tell myself that everything else is a lie my ego is feeding me. I am as God intended, and it is good. And even if you don't believe in God, you can still one hundred percent believe in yourself.

You are so not alone.

We all have negative messages in our heads. Whether it's your mother or your ego, the messages are there. I don't want you to think of ego as me saying you've got a giant one, or that I think you're completely full of yourself, or that I'm only talking to the egomaniacs here. Egomaniacs probably aren't reading this book, and I certainly didn't write any parts of this book with them in mind. But we all have an ego that propagates our fears. The ego takes over where the originator of our negative beliefs leaves off.

The ego works as hard as it needs to in order to keep us separated from our intuition and distanced from our souls. The ego makes us think there are practical ways to get what we want, no spirit needed. The ego tells us we just are lowly beings and that we don't get what we want because we do not deserve it.

As we are united in this problem of ego and negative messages, I want us to be united in defeating them within ourselves and denouncing them forever by living joyful lives. I believe that, if we work hard enough against these negative messages and ego driven thoughts, we can fully reunite with the inner voice that's a connection to who we really are. We all have this voice that belongs to our soul. The more we listen to that voice and whole heartedly embrace it, the happier and more successful, and for sure more peaceful, our lives become. When you feel this sense of relief, contentment, serenity, and joy, you want more of it. Your soul never talks shit about you. God who infuses your soul, never talks shit about you. This is the place we want to permanently reside. Out with the negative. In with the positive. Out with ego, in with spirit. This is how you reacquaint yourself with your purpose, your passion, and your destiny. You cannot hear it talking to you or believe the amazing things you see and feel if your conscious mind is full of crap. When you begin to pay attention and clear out the garbage, you will start to feel the vibration of your soul. It's been waiting for this moment to arise.

The "I don't know how" and "I can't" dilemmas.

The issues that cause us to believe we can't change our situation is not knowing where to begin, waiting for permission/needing approval, a lack of confidence, a lack of support, telling ourselves it's not practical, and choosing what we think is logic over what we feel in our hearts and souls. Sometimes it's a locus of control problem. People with an external locus of control don't believe they have control over what happens in their lives so, correspondingly, they don't think they have the power to change it. People with an internal locus of control believe they have control and can always work harder or smarter to change their situations. There's a whole chapter on this in the next book.

When life piles up on us.

Sometimes we become so disconnected from our hearts, because of what seems like endless difficulties, trauma and setbacks, that we just can't envision anything much different or better than we've had. And what we've had was limited or not very good at all.

The issues are all valid ones. There's no judgment from me. We get to whatever place we find ourselves in through a mix of personality traits, life experiences, the presence or absence of the right teachers, and support. Wherever you are is where you're meant to be, at this moment, but not for long.

Throughout this chapter, I share the many negative messages I've heard in my own head and ones I frequently hear from others. I can tell you there are many more than I have captured here. And what you have may not be so eloquently laid out in the form of words, but you figured it out from what was said and, more importantly, what wasn't.

Inference and deduction.

Sometimes it's not what they actually say that wires your brain to think "not good enough" but what they do, what they don't say and don't do. Years of having a parent or caregiver ignore you, disrespect your feelings and opinions, talk over you or prioritize themselves or others over you, her child, can have the same impact as if your dad told you directly that you're not worthy. Children are hypervigilant in their environments. In infancy, we determine if our needs are being met reliably and predictably, sometimes but not others or not at all so good luck, kid. Children read body language and nonverbal cues before they have language and every day after. And we know when there is a mismatch between what someone is saying and what they are doing. Even if no one specifically stated you're not good enough, you may have been wired to think and believe that.

Now I'm going to tell you how I kick negative self-talk right in the ass and how you can give your own piles of poo the heave ho too.

As with most things, we must begin at the beginning. You must learn the steps before you can perform the dance.

The art and literal fucking magic of....
RECOGNIZE. REFUTE. REPLACE.

Welcome to my 3-step process to turn your ship, or shit—as it may be—around. With a wave of this wand, you will change the negative self-talk into a language of sparkly self-love. Glitter everywhere! The result is magical. You're welcome.

1. Recognize.

I want you to begin to take inventory of how many times a day you say negative and derogatory statements like the ones I mentioned but make sure to jot down all your own.

But how do I even know what the messages are?

Feelings. Your feelings are the expressions of your underlying thoughts and beliefs. Every time you feel frustrated, sad, angry, disappointed, depressed, anxious or worried, I want you to pause.

Excavate. What are you thinking? What part of what you're feeling is the situation itself and what part of it is that you've been triggered? What beliefs about yourself have been brought to the surface?

Most often, it isn't the situation itself that causes us to feel strong emotions but what the situation represents deeper in our minds. This can be true for positive emotions too, but here we are focused on the negative ones. We generally know how to handle the positive feelings just fine. Like, you don't suffer as a result of joy overload. I need a therapist….too much freakin' happiness just isn't a thing. Right? We can handle that one if we're fortunate enough to experience it.

Getting to the core of the emotion.

Recognizing what you are telling yourself is critical. It starts with how you feel. When you feel angry, the anger is the result, but what is the cause? We get pissed off when we perceive that our boundaries have been violated. To get at the root of what's really happening, ask yourself, **"Why do I feel angry about this? Is this situation a trigger for a story I tell myself?"** It's possible that the situation is reinforcing a message you're already saying, such as I'm not good enough or life's not fair. It triggers subconscious memories of other times when you felt not good enough, and you get a snowball effect that commonly starts with anger and ends in sadness and frustration.

The situation itself can make you angry or bummed out but if it lingers and you can't let it go, it's a trigger that's been, well… triggered.

In my life, there are times when I have felt frustrated and angry at my husband over simple things like, recently, when he told me that the plants I bought probably aren't going to do well where I want to plant them and that I've taken too long to get them in the ground. They'll probably die. Now why would I be frustrated and angry about this? He's just sharing his opinion, which I can take or leave and doesn't even require so much as a comment back from me. My anger and frustration are because I was triggered and felt like I wasn't even good enough to pick out plants. Like I can't do anything right. It had nothing to do with him. He doesn't think I can't do anything right. He doesn't think I'm not good enough.

Paying attention to how you feel and linking it to underlying beliefs is a journey.

You might have a lot of shit sandwiches or a few. You have some unknown amount of triggers for these thoughts.

Much of your day may consist of exasperating, soul-stealing messages. They may even be causing you to deflect compliments, diminish your value and understate your contributions. They may dampen the good times, not allowing you to fully appreciate or enjoy the awesomeness in your life. If you have an underlying message of "the other shoe will drop" you won't be able to fully enjoy the good times because your subconscious is reminding you that the rug was often pulled out from under you in the good times. There was another shoe and it dropped.

Even though I used Kate's crazy Jewish mom (her description) quote at the beginning of the chapter that was for humor's sake. I want to make it clear that while she may be crazy (Kate's description) she seems to adore her daughter and I've never seen her tell Kate she's not good enough. And I don't know them personally. But I do look forward to their posts because they're really funny.

Recognizing what you're telling yourself is the key to knowing why you feel the way you do. Changing the conversation is the difference between a life riddled with anxiety, depression, staying stuck, settling for less, or living a life that you crazy love, full of joy, adventure, and satisfaction.

Really. This is a huge, life-fucking-changing deal. How many times a day are you angry, sad, frustrated, hurt, bummed, stressed, confused, and disappointed? How much pain do you have in your body on a daily basis? How much physical or metaphorical weight are you carrying around that doesn't respond to diets or massages?

Recognition is not sufficient, however. You must also refute and replace to receive the benefit of greater peace and happiness. And we're just about to move on to those. But to finish the process of Recognizing…

Keep a journal with you for five days. In addition to documenting at points where you are angry or upset, check in with yourself at several points during the day. Set an alarm on your phone to remind yourself to stop and report. Write about how you feel when you wake up, when you go to sleep, at lunchtime, and at two other points in the day of your choosing. Maybe when you go on break at work or if an event arises and you are feeling strong emotions. Detail how you feel and use good descriptive words. Then tune in and see what you are saying to yourself during these times.

Acknowledge how you feel. Then listen to what you are saying in your mind. Pay close attention to negative language. If you are thinking negative thoughts about someone else, ask yourself, "What is this lashing out telling me about myself? Why do I feel the way I do right now? What memories is this bringing up, and what is the underlying story of those messages?"

Write down the messages, statements, and phrases that your thoughts say directly and indirectly.

And, when you randomly catch yourself saying something unkind about yourself, either out loud or in your head, pinch yourself lightly to ground the awareness.

Let's Refute some shit.

2. Refute.

Here we are officially taking shit sandwiches, any other negative self-talk and doubt off the menu. You control your thoughts, emotions, and actions. Today is the beginning of the new you in your new life. Feel the power, Gorgeous!

Your tasks: (You should know how I feel about not doing your homework- no excuses. Just do it.)
1. List all the shit sandwiches, lies, and other BS reasons why you are NOT who and where you want to be right now. Get extra paper if you need to but list them all. Include everything that came up in the Recognize process in step 1.
2. Under each excuse, write at least 3 reasons why it isn't true. These 3 reasons are why you CAN get where you want to go starting today because you have proof that you have in fact been feeding yourself a load of crap, probably for a long time.

Example: I'm not smart enough. (commonly said by people who think they need one more degree or certification)
1. I'm actually pretty smart. And, being smart enough to help my clients and audience is only 1-part smart and the rest is me being me.

2. I have college degrees and decades of life experience.
3. There isn't much I haven't been able to figure out when I've needed to.

Example: I'm not worthy of having what I want.
1. I've already achieved many things that I've wanted so I must be worthy.
2. I already have the things that mean the most to me: a husband and children, family and friends, whom I love dearly and who love me (so I must be worthy). And we are healthy and safe.
3. When I decide what I want, it tends to show up, often quickly. I decide, act, and get it. I must be worthy.

Fast forward. I'm worthy and I'm good enough.

When we want to change a bad behavior, it's more easily done when we can substitute a better behavior.

3. Replace.

Replace the negative and untrue messages with positive ones. Get them tattooed on your arm if that's what it takes. It's okay if the positive messages make you feel squeamish and uncomfortable at first. It's also acceptable if you roll your eyes when you first begin to recite them. Keep going. Do it anyway. You'll get super comfy with them in time. Do the work, no matter how it feels at first. Things you can say…

1. I am fucking awesome.
2. I have had challenges and overcome them.
3. All is well and all will be well.
4. I am kind. I am smart. I am important. (Borrowed from the movie *The Help* but true for you too!)
5. I am worthy.
6. Today is going to be extraordinary.

The bottom line is…if it isn't true, you have to stop saying it. This is why the refutation is so important. But then replace those statements with something better and truer.

How to keep the negative messages from coming back…perspective is everything.

Here is a sample situation and how you might handle it.
Example:
You're frustrated at work. Your boss doesn't appreciate how hard you work or how much you care about your job, coworkers and the company. You don't earn enough money and you're too busy to use the vacation time you get and if you do use it, you're still checking (and responding to) emails while you're away. There are meetings every day and you don't have time to get your work done during business hours. You're thankful for your job but you know it's sucking the life out of you.

When you feel frustrated, what are you thinking at that moment?

I work so hard, try to do a good job, and no one appreciates me (not good enough). I don't have the skills I need to compete in the job market these days (not good enough). There are no jobs out there where I will have it better or make more money than I make here (hopelessness).

What you can do.
The Fear and Self-Loathing Habit
You continue to subscribe to your shit sandwiches, stay at your shitty job and end up looking decades older than you really are. You develop a self-soothing side hustle called wine, online shopping and Netflix (no chill). You periodically bitch about the situation to your girlfriends who share similar stories. Weeks turn into years. You barely recognize yourself in the mirror. You are teaching your kids that suffering and poor self-soothing is normal. Don't think they don't know. They do.

Or, you could Recognize, Refute and Replace

You remind yourself you are good enough. The company has evolved into a place where no one is happy, and that environment isn't your jam. You love a happy, upbeat and team-oriented workplace and you've heard of family-friendly companies that have that exact environment and great benefits plus flexible schedules. Shazaam! Maybe they're even rescuing puppies or saving the planet. What?! You're good enough because your great annual reviews at your current crappy job say so. It's not your skills or lack of them that caused that workplace to go down the toilet. And, you remember that you like to learn new stuff anyway and you can learn anything. You're betting your sunny smile and winning attitude can get you a new job. And you're going to rely on your gut and your faith in the big U to bring it to you. Shit, maybe it's even time to start your own powered-by-purpose business.

You're good enough. Your job actually sucks.

You're a great mom even though you forgot to wash Johnny's gym uniform for Friday or to arrange for Sally to get to the birthday party on Saturday. You can't drive her because you have to go in (on your day off) to work at your shitty job with a meeting culture where you can't get your work done during the week. But when you get home from said shit job, you're polishing your resume to include a photo of that sunny smile and you're contacting your cousin's ex-sister in law who happens to be an award-winning headhunter. Because you fucking rock.

The right time to persevere.

It will take time and effort to break the habit. You are going to have to work at this day in and day out because you are rewiring your brain to change what you've been thinking for years, possibly decades. If you're still breathing, you can turn it around. Looking for proof is a useful tactic any time you catch yourself serving up poo between two slices of bread.

The better you get at catching yourself saying anything negative, the less you will do it. Listen for the subtleties. If you're not seeing your negative messages right away, get a friend, coach, or therapist to help capture them.

Replace them with empowering statements. Remember, you have no proof of the disempowering ones. In fact, you have evidence to the contrary. You have shown yourself that there is evidence that you are good enough. Go with it.

Once you've started slamming the door on the negative, you must open the windows to let in fresh air. Let's put positive statements in where the negative used to be. Start with "I am good enough." "I am worthy of love, happiness, and everyday joy." Smile at yourself in the bathroom mirror. In fact, smile at everyone.

Your spark has withered under the weight of the abuse. It's still there because it is only extinguished through death. You are now creating a safe space for your soul to emerge and show you who you really are. This is what you've wanted all along but didn't know how to get it. It is why this is the work most worth doing. You really are enough. I promise.

Though I love all the chapters in this book and believe in the power within each one to transform happiness and success, I think this chapter has a particular magic that is more potent than the rest. If you only do one thing in this entire book, work on recognizing, refuting, and replacing the negative messages in your head. Take control. Regain your energy and vitality. I've seen only great and swift results with my clients who do this. For some, it's daily work for weeks and weeks to relieve themselves of entrenched stories. Others seem to need permission to feel happy, and they more quickly let the negative messages go. I can tell you for sure the messages will pop up from time to time to test you. Your brain will attempt to explain some setback, obstacle, or problem with an incorrect association such as "I knew it wouldn't work out," or "I can't do it." You will already have become a master at sending it away, knowing that you will find the way.

You've got this. I'm right here with you.

NOTES

My nana always said if you can't say anything nice, don't say anything at all. She was right.

What I *ridiculously* love in this chapter:

Here's what the voices are saying but they can't say that to me any more:

Affirmation:

I will be kind to others but to myself first.

CHAPTER 4

The "Letting Go" Ceremony: How to Take out the Trash for Rejection Hoarders

"Misery is a communicable disease."
-Martha Graham,
American dancer and choreographer

Oh my gosh, girl. Let's let some shit go!
Jazz hands!
Let's do this.
Forget R-E-S-P-E-C-T (temporarily, of course). Let's L-I-B-E- R-A-T-E. Nope. Can't make that have the same tempo and meter. And that's why Aretha is the QUEEN.

But seriously…

You know how it feels when you take off your bra at the end of the day? Letting shit go is so much better than that.

Bonfire, anyone?

A letting go ceremony releases all the doubts, disappointment, perceived mistakes, failures, shortcomings, wrong turns, and things you don't like about your life prior to today. Write down everything. List all that's happened to you that needs to be shed because it makes you unhappy. Jot down everything that you've done that you wished you could have gotten a do-over. Got something that you feel is the bane of your existence? And just so we're clear about what a "bane of your existence" is, here is the Urban Dictionary (sorry Merriam!) definition of it:

Something that is so disagreeable with your spirit that it feels like its existence might negate yours.

So, this is something that has been lingering and fuck, fuck, fuckity fucking with your ability to feel great about yourself. Some area where you've fallen short, should have tried harder, stuck with it, pushed through obstacles and dare I say it…gotten what you wanted. Or you pushed and pulled with all your might, and it didn't work out anyway. You're going to let go of what you did not pursue—the guy, world travel, the degree, the career, the job— and you've beaten yourself up about it ever since. Here is where we purge what's eating you. The banes of your existence.

If you still want it, go get it. Stop being haunted by how and why it didn't happen before this day right here. If it's something you no longer want, let all of it go. The what along with the how and why.

If you have documents that support these shortcomings, failures, and fuck ups, get them together. If you think your grade point average wasn't good enough in high school or college, write it down or get the transcripts. If you didn't finish your degree, get out your transcripts or other evidence. Maybe you have a rejection letter (or two) from the college you didn't get into but wanted to. Didn't get that job you really wanted, all twenty-two times? Write down the names of the companies.

Don't get me wrong. If it's not still niggling at you, don't bother including it in the ceremony. But be honest with yourself. If it's bugging you inside, let's acknowledge it on paper. That can be burned, shredded, or fed to a goat.

The burn pile.

I had a file box of rejection letters from children's book publishers saying how my work didn't fit with their current lists. I also had transcripts with grades that weren't as great as they might have been if I had been older and wiser when I started college. I have the letters saying that there isn't anything that can be done to allow me to finish my master's degree in business. My school stated that I could finish the classes I need at a university in Florida, but once I moved, they didn't approve the classes. I was told by someone in a position of authority within the graduate business department that I needed to either finish by a certain time or go away for good. She then refused to approve any classes I could take as a replacement for a one credit speech class that had nothing to do with business. My college in Florida where Kent approved for me to finish my few remaining classes, didn't offer this one credit speech class or any other graduate level speech class. I remember, at one point, I sent to the Graduate School of Management office the entire graduate course catalog and said, "Pick anything, I'll take it."

I would have taken chemistry or any graduate English class at that point. My MBA fell apart and remains incomplete over a one credit fucking speech class that coincidently stopped being a requirement in that MBA program at some point after I was told to go away. Not having the paper, the degree, and not having finished what I started and put so much work into has haunted me over the years even though I've long since gone in a different direction. It's left undone, and it appears I can never complete it. So, Jack Canfield, I can't finish what I started with this one. Granted, no one, other than God, can take the knowledge I learned in that MBA program from me, so it isn't wasted. I did want to finish the degree and get the physical acknowledgement of my work, however. I am grateful to Kent for accepting me into that program and for the professors who taught me so much, but the school will never receive a single extra dollar beyond the tuition I paid because of my experience's tragic ending. Don't reward who and what haunts you. I don't want an MBA enough to spend another $30,000 on it; I'm still paying for the last one. I have the knowledge I learned there. I'm happy where I am and with where I'm headed. I'm not going to spend the time, energy, or money to do that one, again. But that experience definitely qualifies as a bane of my existence.

I also have other "regrets" or perceived failures that I've thought about over the years. Not getting into a PhD program in clinical psychology. Staying in positions that were beneath my skill level in the corporate world. Chronically under-earning. Not trying for more challenge and more money. Being too nice and too considerate of others who didn't deserve it and didn't return it. Holding myself back with a disempowering story of an abusive childhood. My childhood happened and is part of my story. It's part of my strength and should never have been disempowering. That was me abusing myself. If this is you, too, let it go.

If it causes you pain, write about it. If you have any lingering shit sandwiches that you want to continue to obliterate, write those down too. Gather everything that is disempowering. If you have been hiding in your clothes, get rid of whatever you've been hiding in. Don't pitch your entire wardrobe so that you have to go buy all new clothes or go to work in pajamas on Monday. Pick a symbolic piece of clothing that is evidence of you hiding, playing small, or showing the world how fucking unconfident you have been. You're going to get rid of it. That you is gone, and a new one's coming out of the cocoon. Just like Taylor Swift says, the old Taylor can't come to the phone right now...cause she's dead.

Do you wonder how some people can feel so confident at such a young age? That's how I feel about Taylor Swift. She's a powerhouse. How does she have her shit together in her twenties? I'm in awe. She gives 200% and seems to really care about her fans. How does that all happen? I hope I get to chat with her at some point and find out. End of the T Swifty digression. Well, not really a digression. I think you get my point.

People, narcissists, abusers, experiences, challenges, illnesses, death, and disappointment change us. OPEs (other people's expectations) change us if we let them. The word "should" can change us if we let it. Fucking fear has a dramatic impact on our lives, dreams, beliefs, and possibilities, if we let it.

You become what you believe you are.

When we believe it, we become it: ugly, fat, disappointing, sad, depressed, stupid, insufficient, inarticulate, a failure, a quitter, or not good enough. None of these were true of any of us until WE decided they were. They're inaccurate conclusions to what has been said and not said, what has been done to us and not done for us, and what has happened or not happened to us. These labels are false conclusions drawn from life experiences, false evidence appearing real. FEAR. And they're easier to believe than positive messages. We were all Taylor Swifts and Meghan Trainors and Beyoncé's inside before we weren't. For some of us, we became a shell of our inner diva quickly through abusive, neglectful, and hurtful childhoods with parents who were narcissists, psychopaths, mentally ill, alcoholics, substance abusers, and victims of domestic violence. For others of us, we abandoned our powerful inner warriors after a series of failures and disappointments that we didn't expect, didn't want, and didn't know how to effectively deal with. We gave up our sassy, self-assured persona because life as it happened didn't match the blueprint we had in our heads in one or more areas of our lives. Your job or career path hasn't turned out to be what you expected in terms of achievement, opportunity, titles, or bank accounts. Your relationships are on repeat and you think Mr. Right, the only remaining one in existence, is hanging out with the unicorns and leprechauns. You've become some version of yourself you barely recognize in the mirror: tired, haggard, exhausted, heavier, out of shape, maybe even with roots showing and shirts with kitties on them. You only wear black, grey, and cream because you're pretty sure you look professional, but they keep you invisible.

At some point, you were vibrant, smiley, and happy. You had some confidence or maybe a lot of it. Your inner archetype was intact. My inner archetype is Athena, the wisest and most courageous daughter of the Greek

God Zeus. She was also purported to be the most resourceful. And Zeus's favorite daughter. I wasn't ever anyone's favorite daughter. And I was the only daughter either of my parents ever had. I suppressed my inner Athena when life piled up on me. I gave her an extended vacation. She's back now. Determine who your archetype is. My best friend Abigail uses Jael, a heroine from the Old Testament of the Bible. Jael killed the enemy (during the wars with the Canaanites) Sisera by offering him respite in her tent, but as he slept, she drove a tent stake through his head and into the ground.

Be very clear: I am NOT advocating, encouraging, or suggesting violence in any way! Not even against perceived enemies or people who have wronged you. I am an extremist in the nonviolence movement. I believe we can be very powerful without harming anyone or anything. I shoo cockroaches out of my house. I don't believe we have the right to hurt anything. I live the COEXIST mantra. Don't get me wrong, the cockroaches can't live in the house with me. There are boundary lines.

Having positive, strong, and powerful role models and inner archetypes will help. Know them. Name them.

We are letting go, in a most ceremonious fashion, of all the stuff that has weighed you down.

Write all your pain, self-inflicted, and externally derived, and gather the "evidence" that supports it. Safely light a fire in your fireplace or firepit. Place the papers in it. Watch the flames. As you watch the smoke and embers floating in the air, give thanks that you are enough. Good enough, smart enough, beautiful, thin, rich, and resourceful enough.

Give thanks that you have had all the right experiences that make you who you're meant to be so that you can do the work you're meant to do. There are no accidents. Don't beat yourself up for beating yourself up. Let it go. Tomorrow is a new day. Give thanks. If you can't burn the papers, cut them into little pieces, shred them, tear them up and donate the clothes that no longer suit you. If Beyoncé wouldn't wear it, neither should you. They are not your truth any longer. Set yourself free.

Continue to give thanks for your own divine wisdom. Give thanks for all your experiences. Give thanks for your intuition. Give thanks for the gifts you have been given. Give thanks for your soul's purpose and ask that you be given the knowledge of this mission and the means to fulfill it. You are enough.

Above all, give thanks for your ability to let it all go. Let go of everything that weighs you down, suffocates you, binds you like a whale bone corset, and causes you to shallow breathe and stand all hunched over. Let go of all you fear. Fuck fear. So worthless unless you are truly in a dangerous situation which we rarely are. Let it all go.

Every morning ceremoniously lift off your shoulders any weight that may have crept back. Place it on the ground. Or offer it up to the sky. Make this part of your ritual so that you can continue to release what you've accidentally picked back up and any new anvils you've decided to carry as well. You will pick shit up again that you've let go of. I know you. You're like me. Your empathic, kind, nurturing, and life's been hard. You will pull some of the stuff back in even after you've burned it. It's ok. Set yourself free again. Let go until the cows come home if need be. If you take on someone else's stuff, set it back down. Give it back to the Earth. If you take up your own stuff again, shit that isn't benefitting you, let it go. Again.

You can be kind but have boundaries.

You can be empathic but drawn the line.

You can be confident and powerful. You once were even if the last time was when you were a child.

I often ask myself, well, what would my daughter Alexa do? Even ten years past the McDonald's drive thru incident, she remains my inspiration for GET WHAT YOU WANT including as recently as last Saturday at our nail appointment. She reminded me that it was okay for me to run next door and grab a coffee so that I could totally luxuriate while getting my mani and pedi. "Get what you want, Mom," she said. And she meant it. She wasn't implying that I be disrespectful and keep the nail techs waiting on me forever. But we've had to wait on the nail techs, even with appointments, and that's part of our collaborative dynamic. We wait on them, and they, most graciously, waited the five or so minutes for me to grab a coffee. I thanked them. And that's why we love them…every two weeks. And thank you Alexa, not only for being my inspiration for teaching women to go from pushover to powerhouse, but for reminding me when I fall back into the old habit. Even when she isn't with me, I can hear her in my head. "Get what you want, Mom."

If you get lost, ask your inner Athena (or whomever you choose) to guide you. Ask her to step forward and show you the way.

And then think…

What would Taylor do? Or Alexa? ☺

Go you.

"In the end what matters most is: How well did you love? How well did you live? How well did you learn to let go?"-
Dalai Lama

NOTES

If it doesn't make you happy, let it go. If it does make you happy, revisit the memory often and for sure, do it again.

What I ridiculously love in this chapter:

Letting Go Ceremony (Insert Date):
What I Will Release:

Affirmation:

I keep the lessons and let go of the pain. I let joy flow through me every day.

CHAPTER 5

Purpose: The 'P' Word You Can't Get Enough of

"Purpose is defined as one's life compass."
Bosco Anthony,
Digital Strategist and inspiring Ted Talk giver

In his Ted Talk titled "Feeling Stuck: Fueling Life from Average to Epic", Bosco Anthony goes on to clarify that your purpose is more important than your name, your country of origin, and your passport.

While much of the material and exercises in this book will help you excavate your purpose, there are a few specifics I want you to understand.

You're perfectly equipped to fulfill your purpose.

In his Ted talk about his #1 bestselling book of all time, A Purpose Driven Life, Rick Warren says your purpose can be found in your gifts. Your gift encompasses your identity, income and influence. He asks the audience, "What's in your hand?" What have you been given and what are you doing with it?

I'm frequently asked, "Are you sure I have a purpose?" Yes, I'm sure you have a purpose. I'm equally sure your life experiences contain the clues and that you have intuition that will serve as your GPS if you listen to it. No one is left out. No one is deselected from having a purpose. Neither is anyone given a free pass to merely consume resources and contribute waste. No one is born without the seeds of a rich life. **You have a purpose and**

it is not only your destiny to fulfill it but your responsibility to do so. The planet is a symbiotic home and we are all responsible to everyone and everything else that occupies this home. We have a role to fulfill and when we fulfill it the world is better. We are better. There is no path to enduring happiness that fails to include fulfilling your life's mission.

Purpose is what gives your life meaning.

Purpose is what gives your life meaning. Some call it your raison d'etre; your reason for being here. Your purpose is where you stop checking boxes, doing the "shoulds," and start living the life that resonates with every single fiber of your being. Your soul knows why you're here. Life does not happen by chance. You came here with a plan.

Your purpose may not be to cure cancer or anything of that magnitude. It does involve helping people, animals, or the planet because everyone's purpose is to serve in some way. It could be creating art for others' enjoyment. It could be doing something that makes a difference within your family or community. It's bigger than yourself. And it is part of the foundation of your enduring happiness. It connects you with your tribe.

"Twenty-three hundred years ago Aristotle concluded that, more than anything else, men and women seek happiness. Much has changed since Aristotle's time. And yet on this most important issue very little has changed in the intervening centuries."
- Mihaly Csikszentmihalyi in Flow

Your purpose has a different vibe.

When you do work that fulfills your purpose, you feel passion and this heightened state raises your energetic vibration. When you operate from this higher frequency, you get "in the zone" or in a state of "flow," where you effortlessly create, excel, and where time passes unnoticed. Angela Duckworth, psychologist, success researcher, and author of the book *Grit: The Power of Passion and Perseverance*, refers to passion as "sustained, enduring devotion" and writes of passion that "enthusiasm is common, endurance is rare." When you find your purpose, you will have endurance and passion. You will have tapped into that which lights you up and it will give you the tenacity and grit to fulfill that which you are called to do.

When I help clients achieve a breakthrough, I feel completely exhilarated. Same for when I write a piece that I think is life changing. And when I get notes from clients and fans telling me that I've helped them change their lives, I'm not even sure sex feels better than that no matter how great the sex is.

I got this note from an amazing woman with whom I got to connect: "Lisa, God is using you to inspire…for the first time in a long time I am excited about the future."

Inspiring, connecting and helping others feel hopeful is what I'm here to do. There's something magical about soul alignment.

Think about your life.

What have you been interested in for a while before you let it go? Being an artist, developing an exercise routine, going pro as an athlete, playing a musical instrument, pursuing a Ph.D.?

When you identify your life's purpose and how you will fulfill it, you'll feel sheer joy and have the endurance needed. You'll know. It's the thing you can't not do.

If you have spans of time where you're "in the zone" or "in flow" and time passes without notice as you effortless create, you're onto something.

I'm not saying the fulfillment of your purpose isn't work. Some days, getting into flow is nearly impossible as distractions abound. But when I'm working on a book or an article, I think about what I want to tell you and I get so excited about it because I know its life changing. On coaching calls when the client meets me in the zone, magic happens, and lives are changed. It's like having pixie dust sprinkled on you and it really allows you to fly.

You must keep going on the days when the words don't flow so easily, or you spend the whole day writing words that may not make any final cut for an article, blog, or book. You may paint for days on a canvass that will never see an exhibit. You may create a plan for a business venture that will never get off the ground. When you are creating in your zone, you create for creation's sake. And in the midst of all you create, there will be some masterpieces. You understand that all time spent in your craft is time well spent honing your skills and learning. When you're fulfilling your purpose, you understand that you must continue to grow even after you've achieved success. And you want to.

Purpose can be simpler than creating art, writing books, excelling at a sport or saving some part of the world. Perhaps you're a connector. Your gift is that you connect people with one another. You may be the glue that holds your family together by organizing family events and making the phone calls that let each person know how the others are doing. You may be an organizer, and because of you, many peoples' lives are easier. Undoubtedly, you're a teacher with the wisdom of the Universe at your beck and call. Perhaps you're a storyteller and disseminate knowledge, useful and trivial, so that you enlighten while entertaining those around you. Minimally, you're a role model just because you live in proximity to other humans who observe your actions and listen to your words. That's a great purpose if you had no other. But you do.

Your home base is your sacred space.

Your home base is like the warm embrace of a beloved grandmother, where you return when you experience a shift that is difficult. It's your center and balance spot. When you lose your job, experience an illness, or the death of a loved one, it's your calming friend. Your home base is that place to which you retreat when you have a difficult day. Setbacks, heartbreak, and obstacles remind us to return to the innermost parts of ourselves, to dig into our cores as we search for meaning in life's challenges, and in a larger way, for meaning in our lives. In the absence of such interruptions, we might be content to power through, failing to take inventory in a deeper way. In the presence of life-altering moments, having had the wind knocked out of us, we are forced to pause.

As we attempt to make sense of the adversity, we are urged to ask ourselves "Am I living according to what gives my life meaning?" It is then that you return to the basics of who you are. The ballet barre is the place to which every ballet dancer, beginners and the most accomplished, returns. For all dancers, the barre is our nurturing mother. She is predictable, comfortable, and yet each day she asks more from us, not letting us reside in the familiarity of years spent side by side. I have learned to find myself on the elliptical machine as well now that I don't take ballet classes anymore. When I'm in the midst of anxiety attacks or depression, I know if I get on the elliptical machine, I'll remember who I am. I can, if only temporarily, shed the atmospheric disturbance that's rattled my natural frequency. I can find myself through whatever difficulties I'm facing. Maybe your home base is nature. Maybe it's in a yoga class. Maybe you find it through journaling, prayer, or meditation. Wherever it is, you need to identify it, so you know where to go to get in touch with the truest, most vulnerable, and authentic parts of yourself. All of yourself. It is then that you find another piece of your purpose.

Discovering Your Purpose Exercise.

How do you begin to figure out your purpose if you don't know what it is?
1. **Announce that you are ready to know your purpose.** You're telling your soul to wake the fuck up and announcing to your conscious self, God, the Universe, whatever your source is called, that **I AM READY**. No one is born without a purpose; it's present from day one and is only extinguished at death, so age doesn't matter. It's not like the cerebral cortex where, if you're younger than twenty-four, it hasn't fully developed yet or like skin, which, if you're in your fifties, has undoubtedly become less plump and may have headed south. Your purpose is a seed planted, lying dormant until the time is right. Ask yourself, "What am I here to do?" and be still so you can hear the answer. Go to your home base and let your authentic self ask for your purpose to step forward. Repeat until the answer feels free to come out.
2. **Look for clues.** Think about experiences you've had in your life that made you happy. What have you done that made you feel fulfilled? Glance back through journals. Look for a running theme in your work, volunteer service, and leisure activities. What did you want to be when you grew up?
3. **Brainstorm.** Give yourself 60 seconds and write down everything you think you'd like to be/do. Don't think about it, quantify it, qualify it as realistic or not, or limit your answers in any way. Just put 60 seconds on a timer and GO! Look for similar qualities in what you've written down. Repeat.
4. **What would you do if there were no obstacles of time, money or energy?** For me, if I had no limitations and could pursue anything I wanted, I'd do what I do now, but I'd get my PhD. And I'd also audition for a character role on Broadway. And I'd write. And spend my in between time eating amazing food and drinking

coffee in the best coffee shops while I travel the world and have conversations with random strangers and collect their stories. I'd document the human experience on a grander scale than I do now.

5. **Prioritize your happiness.** This sounds obvious but most of us don't do it. We put the happiness of our children, our spouse, partner, parents, family, friends and maybe even our coworkers ahead of our own. The truth is that it's much easier to make others happy when we are happy. Then it's more like sharing happiness rather than donating it.

6. **Try stuff.** You will more likely find your purpose through trial and error. Except that there are no errors, only no thank you's. It's great to think about it, meditate on it, and journal these exercises. There is no substitute for experiencing things. That's the most accurate information. So, out of that head and off that couch. Remember, Netflix can wait. Your purpose has been waiting long enough.

7. **Don't take it so seriously that you don't have fun finding it.** Do take it seriously. It's time for you to find what sets your soul on fire! But do also have fun with it like when you walk into a club and find out it's Disco Night. You love the night life, you got to boogie…

8. **Surrender.** It is only when we unclench, let go, stop striving for perfection and shut off our logical, practical brain and remember that what we are searching for is already within us, does it become possible for it to emerge. Let it unfold like the plot the plot twist in Gone Girl or Mulholland Drive. Stop trying to hurry it. Relax on the figuring out the "how it can be possible" of your purpose. Breathe. Release. Suspend your disbelief.

I know you are excited to know. You want to meet your purpose right now. You are awakened and eager. You must remember that you are co-creating with spirit, with an energy and you must be still to hear it. You must surrender the need to "figure it out" and let it come to you. As Gabby Bernstein says, "the Universe has your back."

Feeling the frustration.
Try not to get frustrated if your purpose doesn't come to you right away. I know waiting and putting clues together can be exasperating because you're ready and excited. You may look at the clues and nothing seems to be resonating with you. You may be spending time in your home base and nothing comes. It will come. It may already be trying to speak to you but you're qualifying, criticizing, classifying and judging it with that amazing logical, practical brain of yours. You must be that inner child to let it truly come forward. You must be willing to embrace whatever it is even if it completely violates what you think is sane or possible. Reckless abandon. Dance in the rain. Swim topless. Let your inhibitions and anxieties go. Set the weight down again. Release preconceived notions of how small or grand it will be. Re-release your fears about what your purpose might demand of you in order to fulfill it. Let go of agonizing over the "how" of it all. And journal the fuck out of your thoughts and dreams. It will come to you. I promise.

Fine tuning what you're receiving.

I have known most of my life that I wanted to help people. When I was a younger child, I wanted to be a teacher and a mother to two children. As an adolescent, I wanted to be a movie actress and dancer like Audrey Hepburn. When I wasn't listening to my intuition, I studied business. When I was listening to my intuition, I studied dance, psychology, positive psychology, and coaching. There was a palpable difference in the way I felt studying business and the way I felt studying psychology. With my business classes, I studied and did well because I had decided I would. Psychology was so interesting that I voraciously consumed the material, went to all my classes, asked questions, volunteered as a research assistant, and easily remembered what I heard and read. Helping professions feel so much better to me, a noticeably higher vibration. I have donated money to several charities. I volunteer as a Guardian ad Litem advocate for children. My purpose: I am here to help people (and animals). In a way, I'm a teacher. The current vehicles are writing and coaching, but it wasn't always writing and coaching. It used to be donating money or donating my time, volunteering in my children's classrooms at school. And teaching kids to read and do math. The way you pursue your purpose can change, but your purpose does not. When you pursue your purpose, you feel the passion. How you fulfill your purpose most often comes to you over time, not overnight. How you fulfill it may change as you enter new phases of your life and that's great. Go with the flow.

Why do you need to find your purpose?

You need to find your purpose so that in some way, small or large, you're feeding your soul and feeling truly alive. You need to pursue what sets your soul on fire so you don't experience the long, slow diminishment I refer to as soul death. It's far worse than physical death because you get to observe it and feel the longing for something more, the sobriety of life without dreams, the dismal din of life droning on day to day, living only to the length of it and not to the width of it. You always have regret standing in your shadow waiting to say I told you so.

On the contrary, doing what you are meant to do while you're on this awesome planet raises your energetic vibration. This higher vibration not only feels good, but it changes your physiology, emotions, thoughts, and actions. It rearranges your molecules. Living in that higher vibration even for short periods of time gives you a place to return to when you need to center and rebalance yourself. You know where to go to release stress that doesn't involve a bottle of wine, self-medication, shopping, or other activities that may feel good in the moment but have a nasty boomerang effect.

Begin at the beginning, with stealing time.

Find a way to live your purpose for an hour per week to start if that's what you can highjack from your schedule. Volunteer somewhere that's in line with your purpose. Take a class in something you've wanted to learn. Take time to notice the difference between when you're doing something related to your purpose and everything else you do, such as your job you don't love. Knowing there's an energetic difference and feeling it for yourself is more than half the battle. You'll want more. Your life will become a game of hotter and colder as you encounter people and activities that are closer to your purpose or farther away.

If you aren't super sensitive to energy naturally or because you've dulled your ability over time by doing things you don't love, keeping company with people you don't like, or tolerating and settling, don't worry. You can increase your sensitivity to energy by focusing on it. When you're sitting with friends, mentally duck out of the conversation for a few minutes. Step outside the situation and listen in as if you happen to be passing by. How does it feel? What's the vibration of each person, of the conversation? Does it feel authentic to you and your purpose? Is it where you want to be or simply where you are now?

This conversation may be making you uncomfortable. Human nature is to seek what's familiar and comfortable, even if it's not good for you, such as staying in abusive or controlling relationships, losing years at a job you don't love, or where your talent is not valued. You will make endless excuses about why you don't do what's best for you. You'll settle. You'll drown out that inner calling, turning down the flame until it's a tiny spark. Your purpose is only extinguished with physical death; however, you can live your entire life in a state of soul death. Soul death is when you continue to live in a life that is inconsistent with your reason for being here. You become dead inside even if you mask it on the outside. You can do it for a day, years or an entire lifetime. Don't let anything outside yourself guide your life.

Be your own bullshit meter. If you think you have a situation where you're not making excuses for yourself and have a legit reason why you can't do something, email me. I have been coached by seriously good bullshit slayers. Turns out, I'm a natural at it too. This is one of my favorite quotes, attributed to E.C. McKenzie, but I've also seen versions of it attributed to other people:

"The man who really wants to do something finds a way, the other man finds an excuse."

Look at Elon Musk. The guy is 48 years old (2019) and has several companies that do things like build rocket ships and energy efficient cars. Don't you think plenty of people told him he can't or that's impossible… on just about everything he's ever done? The difference is that he doesn't let that stop him. He finds a way.

Embracing your purpose like an old friend.

Whatever your life's purpose is, it's needed. There are no accidents, duplicates, or frivolously awarded human potential. You are given the exact experiences you need to fulfill the purpose you were born with. Your job is to do it. Trust that whatever you need along the way will show up. You don't need to know how. You don't need to see the whole staircase. Just take the first step. If you have faith, lean into it. You cannot have faith and fear in the same moment. It's one or the other. Choose faith and fear disappears.

As a writer, who has degrees in other things but not writing, I've told myself that it's pretty presumptuous to want to be a *New York Times* best-selling author, on that coveted list with talented writers who have spent years and loads of tuition money studying the craft. How dare I think I should be on the same esteemed list as them? I have a cousin who's a supremely talented journalist and writer. He has an undergraduate degree in journalism and a masters from Columbia in Creative Writing. How dare I put myself in his field? Isn't it insulting to all the writers I love who studied writing? Maybe. But it's my big dream anyway.

I have studied the craft now and continue to bit by bit, not at a university. I've taken Malcolm Gladwell's master class. James Patterson's too, even though I don't write fiction. I studied in a writer's group. I've worked with a book coach and a storytelling coach while writing this book. Because I care as much about the writing and making this book worthy of your time and the NY Times best sellers list, the teachers have shown up. My besties have read parts of this book and said, "Yeah, it's good. But it's not you. It's not like hanging out with you. You're so witty and funny." I knew then and there that I needed to work harder. The book was mostly finished at that point. But it wasn't good enough. I want you to feel like you're hanging out with me. We're having cocktails and talking about life and happiness and dreams (oh my!). Voila, storytelling coach appears. The place, American Stage, where I took an Improv comedy class last fall offers a storytelling class. I signed up for it. The class got canceled because of low enrollment. I got a refund and promptly emailed one of the instructors and asked her to work with me privately. She did. The one on one attention I've gotten for nearly the same amount of money has added superpowers to my storytelling and the feel of this book. And set me up nicely to write a memoir in the future, which is another dream on my horizon. There are no accidents or coincidences. Life unfolds exactly as it's meant to. You can't rush it and you're not late.

Do not worry one bit about how it will happen. I know our amazing big brains like to figure out the details and we feel super frustrated when we can't figure it all out. I can tell you for sure, when you are crystal clear about what your dream is and you're willing to do whatever work it takes, you are opening the vault of resources supplied in short order by unseen forces acting on your behalf.

> *"I used to think there must be thousands of girls sitting alone like me, dreaming of becoming a movie star. But I'm not going to worry about them. I'm dreaming the hardest."*
> *-Marilyn Monroe from her autobiography <u>My Story</u>*

You don't need to know how. You just need to dream hard. And I've dreamed so hard about being a successful writer so that my reach is millions of people who need my knowledge and the hope and inspiration I can give you. I can't worry about everyone or even anyone else dreaming my dream. I'm dreaming the hardest. Just like Marilyn. So, no limiting our big dreams. Right? Right. You want it. Go get it.

One more word about your purpose before I move on. Yes, I'm absolutely certain you have one. No, I'm not wrong. Everyone comes into this world with a purpose that your soul knows. Your purpose is simple. The way you fulfill it may be more complex, or not. The way you fulfill it may change as you move through life. The purpose remains the same and is as constant and present as your DNA. If you sit quietly, you will hear it. You may have to sit still more than once. Quiet your mind and let your heart speak. It's been waiting to talk to you.

NOTES

It isn't the truth that sets you free, it's your purpose, that which gives your life the greatest meaning.

What I *ridiculously* love in this chapter:

What small steps will I take this week to find my purpose:

Affirmation:

I honor my calling and know the steps are being shown to me now.

CHAPTER 6

But What Do I Want? How to Find What You Want When All You Know Is That You Don't Have It Right Now

---

"What you do makes a difference, and you have to decide what kind of difference you want to make."
-*Jane Goodall,*
scientist, conservationist, peacemaker, mother nature

What do I want to do?

What do I want to have?

Who do I want to become?

Clues from the present.

In chapter one you essentially placed clues into five columns. What you love, like, tolerate and dislike point you in the direction of what you want to do and have. You want to do and have more of what you love and like and less of what you tolerate and dislike. As you become more aware of what you love and like, add items to your lists. When you do the exercises in this book, you become more cognizant of what is pleasing and not so enjoyable. Awareness creates more awareness. It's kind of like waking up and rubbing the sleep out of your eyes and the world comes into focus. But way more fun than that.

In chapter six we will identify role models which also provide you with clues from the present and possibly the past. Role models and why you admire them reveal clues about who and what you want to become as well as what you want to do and have.

Clues in the past.
I have no idea what I want to be when I grow up.
Have you said that lately? I've heard teens, 20, 30, 40 and 50-somethings and even a few 60-somethings say it. In fact, the only group of people not saying it are kids…who seem to always be able to tell you what they want to be when they grow up! That knowledge seems to go to shit sometime after adolescence for many of us. I found myself, as a teenager, envying kids who knew exactly what they wanted to become. One of my closest friends in high school, Julie, knew she was going to go to college, major in political science, then go to law school and become a lawyer. She wanted to eventually become a politician. She changed her mind about the politician part but, otherwise, did exactly what she said. My friend, Elaina, studied dance her whole life and wanted to become a professional dancer which she did, after training at a conservatory, and my friend, Amy, became a special education teacher which is what she felt passionately about. My husband became an architect, the only thing he ever wanted to be. He took drafting classes in high school. He got two degrees in architecture and has spent the last 25 years working as an architect.

The girl who could not make up her mind.
I, on the other hand, majored in ballet, then business twice, then psychology. Then studied coaching, psychology again, and positive psychology. I

also had nearly enough credits to have minored in French, dance and fashion. I think I could easily have become a psychologist and been fabulously happy as a fashion stylist, fashion historian, a costume designer for movies, a French interpreter, or fitness instructor. I like so many things more than just a little bit.

But she knows what she is not...

It's just as important to look for clues in what you don't like, don't want to be, and don't want to have as it is to look for them in the things you like and love. I know that I can't stand the sight of bodily fluids, so most careers in the medical field are out of the question. If I saw a broken bone protruding through someone's leg, I'd vomit. Brains escaping a fractured skull equals hurl all over the place. You get the idea. I also know what I don't want to do and have like so many commitments I feel exhausted all the time. I love to stay busy and work on that bucket list, but I don't want to be stretched too thin. I don't want to feel stressed out. I have anxiety disorder. I take care of my mental, emotional, spiritual and physical health so I feel less tense. I don't want to live paycheck to paycheck. I know how to do it and I did it for many years, but I don't like it and don't want to do it anymore, so I take steps to avoid it.

She's tough but she's a highly sensitive one.

I know that I feel overwhelmed in loud, chaotic, and crowded environments, so working in an amusement park, stock exchange, or a daycare center is a no for me. I know that I don't love rigid rules, micromanagement, and when everything is too much the same from day to day. So, no factories and no to most corporate jobs. Ha! Where was that tidbit of insight when I was accumulating massive student loans in undergraduate and graduate school for business? I also know now, that narcissists are a deal breaker especially as bosses because I'm a team player but don't want to deal with one person who takes all the credit and none of the blame. I don't love when you're talking to someone and you can tell that they aren't listening because they're thinking about what they want to say next, and it's always about them.

She's clueless. Ugh. As if.

I strongly dislike fluff, nonsense, too much politics, and focusing on shit that doesn't matter, like endless meetings that don't solve any problems. As you may know, these are things commonly found in corporate environments. So why did I ever major in business at not just the bachelor's level but graduate school too? Literally, because I was clueless. And that's why I'm teaching you the importance of looking for clues. The more you know about yourself, the more success you will have in creating a life you ridiculously love. Why didn't I study psychology or social work from the beginning? Because I was clueless. I didn't know anything about who I was when I picked business. I just knew I wasn't going to be a ballet dancer. And that I needed a new major. I didn't know that I'm a highly sensitive person who wouldn't be able to settle for something she didn't hate or for something she happened to be good at. I didn't know that it would be essential to my health and happiness to do something I loved. I didn't know that I would relentlessly pursue happiness, as a woman walking out of the darkness of childhood and into the light. I'd for sure never heard the words lightworker, empath, or healer, and even if I'd had, I would have thought it was woo-woo fluffy stuff.

Unfortunately, when we pick a career path, we usually don't know shit about ourselves. Some people go through life without knowing themselves well which makes finding happiness difficult at best. Or they think because they picked a path that they must stick with it, especially if they're paying back a mountain of student loans. If you're not happy, look for clues. Change your course. And change yourself. Happiness is what life's all about. It's the ultimate pursuit. It's the only pursuit that matters. If you didn't find it at first, find it at last.

Finding happiness isn't rocket science. Happiness feels really good.
The Look for Clues in Your Childhood Exercise.

There is often valuable information about yourself if you look back to your childhood. **What were you like as a child?** Quiet, shy, class clown, the life of the party? **What did you want to become? What did you play when you were alone and with friends? What dreams did you have then? What were your favorite subjects in school? What were you naturally good at?** There are clues in the answers to these questions.

As part of my research, I interviewed women in different parts of the world and in the age ranges from 20's-60's. I also verified that kids can always tell you what they want to be when they grow up. Here are what some of my interviewees recalled wanting to be when they grew up:

Dante: 10 years old; kicker on a professional football team. A kicker because then you still get to play the game, but you don't have guys plowing you over because I'm little.

Samantha: 8 years old; chef in an Italian restaurant, dentist, mechanical engineer, and pediatrician. She acknowledges that it will be tough to be all of them at once but that's the goal.

Catriona: (as a kid) "a singing, dancing Harvard-trained lawyer living in Las Vegas"; Cat is a 20 something, married mother of 5-year-old twin boys, with undergraduate and graduate degrees in English. She currently works as a technical designer for educational software programs. Her five-year plan, however, is to be a published author and to be working for a university. How did she get there from singing, dancing lawyer? Her high school English teacher. According to Cat, "She got me. She taught in a way that really resonated with me." Catriona double majored, not at Harvard, in English and Political Science but realized quickly that political science wasn't what she thought it would be. She stated, in looking back, that she always loved words. Clues.

Danika: (as a kid) doctor, travel/tour guide, jet pilot, architect, sea captain, ocean researcher. Danika is in her 40's and works as a German-English translator. She also works as an entrepreneur, business coach and writer. Danika has traveled the world and still feels like she may do something with her tour guide passion. She knows she feels most at home by the sea or on it. She still smiles at the thought of being a jet pilot. While she didn't immediately become any of her childhood dreams, she's a self-proclaimed go-getter and when she gets inspired, she takes action. Clues. And action.

Really dig deep. Go on a mental journey of your childhood and think about what mattered to you. All of it. **Who did you idolize and, more importantly, why? What were your loves? What did you love about them? What did you want to be?**

Whether you grew up in the age of the internet and Google, with fast access to information about everything and everyone, or not, this process is the same. **Who did you love, what did you want to do, and what did you love about it?**

Are there any connections you can make about then and what you love now?

I can look at it now and clearly see that I wanted to make a big impact, reach millions of people, and be adored. I wanted to be loved. I never dreamt of winning the lottery or marrying a wealthy man. I wanted to give something big to get what I wanted. And I wanted to be rich. I wanted all the things money could buy: travel, clothes, jewels, fancy restaurants, cars, big beautiful houses, all of it. I always wanted all those things but somehow along the way, poverty settled in hard and made me think that I would always be poor, live in a small house, and consider life good if I had enough food to eat. Maybe get to take a trip or two. Somewhere along the way, I became disconnected from what I wanted. As I began to have more, a life out of my mother's house, a husband, a job, and a family of my own, I knew I wanted money, travel, and beautiful shoes, but I needed to take great care of my family first. Who I wanted to become and what

I wanted to do and have took a back seat. Family first. I heard this from Catriona and several of the women I interviewed, many of whom are now midlife and pursuing their dreams. Having an amazing husband and kids, compared to where I'd been, made me feel like I'd hit the fucking jackpot. I did want more. But I focused on raising my kids and living life on a daily basis, grabbing a wee bit of luxury where I could: old Mercedes sedan, trip to Europe, weekend getaways, dining out occasionally, and buying lots of clothes for my kids. I never really changed what I wanted, luxury and impact, but I did come out of alignment with it for a bit.

I didn't want those things any way I could get them or I would've stayed in corporate America. I needed the alignment of purpose and passion. But not just purpose and passion. I wanted it all. As Marie Forleo says, "make money and change the world." It's ok to want what you want. It's even better to get it. Change the world. Make bank. Be an awesome human.

When you stop dreaming the hardest, your dream slips away and a practical life sneaks in.

Fast forward.

Hindsight gets the last laugh with me, as it so often has. I am a teacher in that I write and coach people on how to be happier and create a life they love. I'm a mother of two children. I'm a prolific writer. My thoughts tend to come in book titles. Even though I still see choreography in my head with certain songs, I have a writer's soul. It turns out that business and psychology are a perfect combination of knowledge to become a great coach and author. Someone who documents the human condition while working to improve it. I understand behavior and how to strategize and come up with measurable goals and plans. Dance requires a level of dedication, commitment, and sheer grit that leaves out anyone who could possibly dream even for a moment of doing anything else. Those that become dancers quite literally must do it. I know that feeling and recognize it again in my need to write. The words choose me; I do not consciously choose them. But I'm happy they are persistent and knew more about me when

I knew little about myself. And when I think about the immensity of all the writers out there wanting to be *New York Times* bestselling authors, I remind myself that I'm dreaming the hardest about it.

The answers to the questions in bold in this chapter are the difference between a nice trip down memory lane and putting together the puzzle pieces of who you are meant to be and what that fabulous babe does.

Was there something you wanted to be but chose a different career for practicality, ease, because you were clueless, or some other reason? What did you want to become before someone (including yourself) convinced you that you couldn't or shouldn't do it?

How does it feel in your gut when you think about it now?

Look everywhere. Do Google searches on jobs that interest you or appeal to you for some reason. **Are there clues in the volunteer work you've done? Do you have a totally new idea? What are your goals in addition to "Be Happy"? Do you want to make a certain amount of money, have a desire to help others, want to start your own business or switch careers? What's your timeline?** You will have a goal to "Be Happy" but what other goals do you have? We will work on one big goal at a time, in addition to happiness.

As with most of the work in this book, this exercise is part cerebral in remembering and examining your life but also intuitive because you must run the gut test on all that you recall so you can tell the difference between what still resonates with you and may truly be part of your purpose and what was just a fad, kid dream, or passing interest.

Use your intuition. You have it for a reason.

A girl can make her dreams come true if she has memory, imagination, and intuition. And really more of the latter two. You will also need action and tenacity and be willing to take risks, do things that others will think is impractical if not outright crazy.

Ask yourself the right questions. Talk to people who do what you think you might want to do.

If you think you want to have a doggy daycare, call up or stop in and talk to at least 5 different dog daycare owners and find out what they love about their businesses and what they wish they knew before they started.

Do your homework. Ask a lot of people a lot of questions so you get a good sample for your feedback.

If you feel like this work is too much for you or you find yourself procrastinating on it, ask yourself why. What objections are coming up around you moving in a new direction?

Thinking about making your dreams come true and doing the early work can feel overwhelming at times. Give yourself that space. Sit with it. Meditate on it and see what comes up for you. Ask the discomfort questions. Is it that you're not ready or that you're feeling the "Holy shit! I can do this" mixed with the fear of "What if it doesn't work?" It's a roller coaster of excitement, hopefulness, fear, and feeling overwhelmed. Get used to it. This is par for the course with any major change you make. And if you want to be an entrepreneur, well, this is life. Entrepreneurship is fantastic, and I never have any regrets about my husband's and my choice to ditch our 9-5s, but it's a roller coaster.

Make a list of what still resonates with you and why. How can this impact or influence your next phase?

So, we're moving forward, putting together the pieces of who you are, what work will set your soul on fire, and what a life you ridiculously love looks like. You've written down your loves, likes on down to complete deal breakers and know the importance of loading your life with loves and likes and unloading your life of the rest.

More clues are found in retrospect as you think about what wanted to be when you were a child and aspects of what you liked about jobs you've had and what you didn't like. Perhaps the best part about looking for clues is that you are sending a signal to God, the Universe, or whomever, that you are ready for signs. You get what you focus on. When you are ready to figure out the new you and new life, the resources will come.

#Signsplease. #Thankyou.

And, if you think the sign is for you. It is. This is how the big U works. On the day that you need it, someone else does too. You will all drive by the sign and see it. Yes, it's for you. Write it down, so you don't forget about it. You will forget it even if it was monumental the day you saw it. Write it down and watch the magical manifesting moments stack up. There is power in seeing the collection of events that are sent your way. You'll find yourself in conversations with strangers who say something random but related to your search. Yes, it's a sign for you. A random conversation with a stranger who tells you something that moves you down the path. Yes, it's for you. Line in a movie or book that strikes a chord. It's for you. Write it down. Keep a journal with you or use the notes on your phone. You'll be surprised how often magic moments happen when you open yourself up to them. All you need to know is ask for signs and say please and thank you. Or, Thank you, next!

NOTES

Simple pleasures and lots of sparkle. Who doesn't want that?

What I *ridiculously* love in this chapter:

What I know I want:

What small steps will I take this week to get what I want?

Affirmation:

I live in an abundant Universe. What I want wants me. With more I do more to help others.

CHAPTER 7

Know Your Role Models. Also Known As, How Not to Reinvent the Wheel Because Oh, by the Way, Wheels Exist

"The most important single influence in the life of a person is another person…who is worthy of emulation."
-Paul D. Shafer,
Author

Role model: a person whose behavior in a particular role is imitated by others (source: Merriam Webster)

I'm going to expand Merriam's definition and say that a role model is someone with whom you feel a palpable connection because he or she is reflecting back to you some part of who you are, who you want to become and what you want to have and achieve. Role models illuminate bits of who we are inside and where we are destined to go. These are people you hope would be proud of you if they knew you. You want to become the person your role models will want to hang out and have cocktails with. Or coffee. Water. Whatever. You want them to want to be around you.

Finding Tony and, in a way, myself.

Here's an example of a role model. Between 2007 and 2009 I was applying to PhD programs in clinical psychology (and being rejected by them). I turned on the television one day after work and Oprah was interviewing Tony Robbins. As I listened to him talk so passionately about how he helps people change their lives from desperate places to very hopeful ones, I felt a vibration in my body. I couldn't not listen to him. I knew I was looking at part of myself. He was showing me, in that moment, something about my destiny. I wanted to help people like that. Not as a therapist. I wanted Tony's kind of connection with those I help. I wanted to be able to use whatever I have in my book learning, experience, and soul to help others and not the limited resources that you're afforded as a therapist. I wanted to focus on what's right about people and not what's wrong with them. I never applied to another PhD program. I went on to complete coach training with Tony Robbins institute over the next few years and have happily lived and worked as a coach ever since.

Why you're there isn't always why you think you are.

I had a similar experience when I was working in 2004 as a special education teacher helping kids get to grade level in reading and math. I worked with kindergarten children. I was frustrated by the limited toolkit I had at my disposal. I wanted to know what was happening in these kids' brains. I decided to take a couple psychology classes at the local university. As destiny would have it, I had to take an introduction to psychology class before I was permitted to take the classes I wanted. In that first class I met a role model who would change my life forever. The professor, who might have been jaded teaching this most basic class, instead, exuded passion for the subject. When he defined psychology as the study of why we think, act and feel the way we do, I was hooked. I felt a vibration. I knew I was looking at part of my life. I never felt that way with any of my business professors or classes in undergraduate or graduate school. One or two psychology classes turned into a second bachelor's degree followed by applications to PhD programs as well as a research assistantship and later paid positions with the professor who became a friend and changed my life. In fact, I worked with him on and off for nearly fifteen years and until very recently.

You must not only see with your eyes and listen with your ears but feel with your soul. Then be willing to fearlessly follow that internal guidance. Better yet, get excited by this new information, eager to see where it takes you. You don't need to see the whole path to take the first step.

Who are your role models?

I know you may have never thought about your role models, much less identified them. Your initial response to the question might be "I don't know" or "I don't have any." Western culture, the only culture with which I have personal knowledge, doesn't really focus on identifying our role models. We don't tap into the wisdom of our elders. We've lost our thirst for the knowledge of those on whose shoulders we stand, if we've even bothered to identify whose shoulders those are. We have become an individualistic society which makes us think we're always going it alone. That it's up to you singularly to make it or not. And we know that everyone is busy, and we fear rejection- that they might not engage with us if we ask. Rather, we spend exhaustive hours reinventing the wheel when, as you know, wheels exist. We're so alone that it doesn't even occur to us that we're working much harder than necessary. And we rarely seek that unbiased perspective that tells us, woman, wheels exist. What are you going to do with that wheel that customizes it and makes it your own?

There are clues about who you are, about your purpose and about your life's work in your chosen role models.

10,000 gurus.

Sometimes, in attempt to figure things out on our own, we encounter a different problem. Rather than operating in isolation, we seek the advice of the masters. All of them. Countless sages. Endless experts. We get so overloaded with everyone else's opinions about the right way to do something that we lose touch with our own internal guidance system. We try this and do that and wonder why we are no closer to making our goal a reality. We imbibe free advice nearly as continuously as we breathe air- scrolling through social media posts, reading books, listening to podcasts, skimming blog posts and articles. Then there are the ascended masters that we know, love and trust and, therefore, shell out precious bank (or credit) for their inside scoop. What you really want is two things: for her to notice you and help you along personally and two, for him to give you the magic bit of stardust wisdom that radically transforms your business and life.

I'm not where I want to be so, bring on more experts.

What we've tried isn't working so we seek more advice…more gurus. Thoughts freefall to thinking maybe we're on the wrong path. Maybe we've made a mistake. It's all been done before! I'll never be as good as the leaders. I'll never even stand out from the pack. Worse still, you might be thinking you don't have what it takes to succeed! How am I doing? Can you relate? There are two problems that occur in listening to too many authorities. The first is information overload, which leads to being overwhelmed, confused, and exhausted. This overload might cause you to walk away from what you love for a while. The second is that you lose touch with your own intuition. You forget that, above all, you must trust yourself. And that's hard to do. It's so easy to learn more and more and more. Betting on yourself, well that's a different story.

Experts are not the same as role models.

Finding your role models requires you to be in touch with your intuition. You're not choosing role models solely with your conscious mind, you must feel the vibration. You select role models because they show you bits of yourself. Role models teach you about who you are and who you are becoming. **Role models show you pieces of what you want to do, be, and have.** They may be people you know or people you've never met and only read about. The goal is not to become secondary versions of these other people but to let them guide you. They already possess qualities you want to more fully develop and express. They have built what you want to build in one way or another. They exhibit traits that have allowed them to achieve in ways that you want to. To find them, however, you must feel the resonance. Then you must ask yourself: "What do I like about him?" "What am I drawn to?" "What must I learn from her?"

Anti-role models.

> "From the errors of others, a wise man corrects his own."
> -Publilius Syrus
> *Roman slave, Syrian, writer 85BC*

You may have a role model who shows you what you don't want to be, do or have.

Having grown up with a mom with issues such as depression, anxiety, substance abuse, alcoholism, and who was mentally and emotionally abusive, I could easily have become someone quite different than the happy, positive, optimistic, empathic person I am.

I loved my mom despite the misery of our life together, even before I understood her issues. I sought love and approval from her as children always do. But I never resonated with her. I didn't ever feel like I was looking at part of myself. We're both introverts and have issues with anxiety and depression, but our lives could not be more different.

I have always managed my issues completely differently than she did. I feel blessed that I have what it takes to do just that. I've known all along how to find positive resources such as exercise, therapy, nature, and helping others. I've never backed down from taking responsibility for my actions or their consequences. I've never resorted to self-medication, seclusion, or reckless behavior. She was my role model for what I didn't want to do and how I didn't want to view the world or interact with it. I am as grateful for what she taught me as my anti role model as I am to all those who've inspired me and changed my life in directly positive ways. I'm not sure I'd be who I am or as committed as I am to spreading compassion and helping others if I hadn't witnessed her intense battles with life.

Relationship role models.

In 1979, my nana remarried, and she and my (new) pop showed me what a happy, healthy, romantic relationship looked like. I had never seen anything like it! You could always see that they adored each other in the looks, the handholding, the respect, and the many thoughtful things they did for each other without being asked. They didn't agree on everything, and they each had their own interests and activities but they looked forward to seeing each other every day. That has always been my benchmark for how I need my relationship with my husband to be. I look forward to seeing him every day. My nana passed away in 1996, way before I could ever imagine living without her, but she is and always will be my role model for much of who I am as a person and how I want to be in all my relationships. I'm here to help others, just as she did. And I choose happiness, just as she did. Even though they're no longer living, my nana and pop have remained my role models for relationships and for how to be good, caring, compassionate human beings.

Career and work role models.

For my work, I have several role models who show me aspects of who I want to be and what I want to achieve. Tony Robbins, first and foremost, has taught me how I want to be as a coach in terms of style and methodology, and he reflects my core values in many ways as a kind-hearted human, making a difference in the world. His intention is to help people change their lives, even if you must lead them back from disaster. However, I don't want to lead 50-hour seminars or get people to walk on fire, even if I appreciate why he does what he does. Tony Robbins and Oprah Winfrey are my role models and mentors for many things. They taught me to stay in my lane and that being in service to others who want to live their best lives is a worthy mission that can also bring me other things I want in my life such as wealth, travel, and many more opportunities to help people, animals, and the planet. We genuinely want to make the planet a better place. They, too, have risen out of the adversity of their childhoods and made amazing lives for themselves. I think it's safe to say they have created lives they ridiculously love. And that's what I'm all about. I've never chewed gum in public since Oprah said not to on the Oprah Winfrey Show back in the 90's. Even though her abhorrence of the sticky substance stems from childhood, she's right about not chewing it. No one ever looks good chewing gum. No gum because Oprah says. Mother Maya (Angelou) didn't curse or drink… at some point, I may work on those.

The bottom line.

If you want to be the next Stephen King, try writing to the current one. In two seconds, I found a message board at www.stephenking.com and his Twitter account @StephenKing. Read every interview you can find where he is being asked questions.

One of two things will happen: you will get a reply, or you won't. If you really want to be a King-like horror writer turned script writer, put his picture on your vision board. If Mr. King doesn't respond, try someone else. If it's something you really want to be, do or have, find a way and don't take no for an answer. Be polite and patient but affirm exactly what you want.

If you want to be a life coach, figure out who your role models are. Contact them but do your homework first. Figure out exactly what you want from each person and what you are prepared to offer in exchange. Affirm it every single day.

Use your resources; you are not alone.

Part of truly becoming the most authentic version of yourself, with your purpose and passion, with your very soul leading the way to a fulfilled life, is to know in whose footprints you are walking.

Role models for everything?

Hella yeah. Remember don't reinvent the wheel. That'd be so much work! I don't have time for that. You don't either.

What *she's* wearing.

I have several fashion role models: Cindy Crawford for her effortless style… button down shirt, jeans, heels or flats, and tailored jacket. Iris Apfel, Judith Maria Bradley, and Maye Musk who are all older women who are incredibly fashionable, vibrant, and beautiful. Judith and Maye are both models at 71 and 70, respectively, and while Maye has modeled for 50 years, Judith began modeling at age 69. Fashion icons. Iris, who is 96 years young, is also my role model for living life. If you look up joie de vivre in the dictionary, I'm fairly certain you will see Ms. Apfel's picture, undoubtedly wearing her big bold glasses and some gorgeous baubles. What I love about Iris is that she's not done! She works and lives…because she has more that she wants to create, most recently a line of big, bold jewelry which is definitely her style, and she wears it with authority. I hope that one day I'm a style icon like her. She says age is a number that it doesn't mean anything, and I couldn't agree more.

Yeah, that life.
I have role models for lifestyle...people who seem to really know how to balance work and everything else like self-care, family, travel, and the pursuit of happiness. My friend, Lori, does this well. She goes to the gym because that's what she needs for herself. She prioritizes family first but also has a job to which she devotes more than 40 hours a week, and she takes pride in what she does. She takes great care of her house and still finds time to play with her awesome hubs and friends often, including trips and weekend getaways. Lori gets an A+ for balancing life. Luckily, I'm one of those friends who travels with her and occasionally meets her at the gym. And, I'm learning to prioritize my own self-care and find the balance.

Following their lead.
I also have role models for things like how not to worry (my husband) and how to go with the flow (my kids), for how to evaluate the risks vs. rewards, and decide if something's worth doing (my daughter).

The secret to getting where you want to go is not being entrenched where you are or in who you are right now.

Whole, not perfect.
In the *Dark Side of the Light Chasers*, Debbie Ford talks about our shadow selves which are repressed parts of ourselves that we suppress because we don't want to identify with them. For example, I repressed anything about myself that I thought was selfish. I'm a caregiver, a nurturer, and a teacher. I'm proud of those parts of me. But what happened as an effect of squashing my selfish side is that I became someone with poor boundaries and almost no self-care. Self-care seemed selfish, and I couldn't see how it wasn't. I've been on a plane many times and heard the whole oxygen mask spiel about putting on your own mask first. Somehow, I never let that generalize to life off a plane for my first three and a half decades. Debbie states, "When we understand that each and every aspect of our humanity

is imperative to feel whole, we take the evolutionary leap into self-love and living our most authentic life. It is in this vulnerable place that authenticity is natural."

KNOW YOUR ROLE MODELS EXERCISE. (Part I)
Where to begin.
1. **Listen your gut. And do the work to be in touch with it.** Be still, be silent, meditate, journal or whatever it takes to turn up your intuition to full tilt.
2. **Give your intuition the top priority over your logical practical brain.** I mean, take your brain with you but don't let it have the loudest voice in your life.
3. **Observe.** This requires you to be calm and quiet as well. Just be. People watch. Listen without thinking about what you want to say next. In fact, don't think about anything at all!
4. **Put yourself in places you don't normally go.** Get outside your normal routine, habits, and path and go somewhere new. And when you get there, listen and observe.
5. **Try stuff. If it appeals to you, try it.** Use that internal GPS. And don't put it off. If it's calling to you, do it.
6. **Look for micro bits of information.** Role models show you behaviors, new ways of thinking and help you recognize the pieces of yourself you've hidden away or with whom you've not yet gotten acquainted.
7. **Learn new things.** You never know why you're in a place. It may not be what you think. It may be to meet someone who will forever change your life for the better.
8. **Follow the feeling.** Trust your intuition. Here's the more difficult part. Hear it. Then following it like it's your job. Take the chance. Tell that practical brain to shush.

> "The morning breeze has secrets to tell you. Do not go back to sleep."
>
> -Wayne Dyer,
>
> *author, motivational speaker and major compassionista*

Know Your Role Models Exercise. (Part II)

Grab that journal or paper and once again, make five columns with the following labels: **Self, Love, Friends, Career, Work**.

Who has inspired you in the past and who inspires you now in each of these areas? **Who are two friends that you admire that you know have each other's backs in a "she'll drop what she's doing if the other needs her" kind of way? Who do you know that can keep each other's secrets? Who will be happy for the other one even when things aren't going well for her? Who lacks jealousy and feels empathy? Who is doing work you could see yourself doing in some way? Who are your relationship role models?**

Who shows you bits about who you are, how you want to feel, and who you want to become?

If you have not identified your role models for yourself, love, friendships, relationships, and career, do so now. Figure out who is where you want to be in each area and figure out how they got there. Why do you feel a resonance with them? What traits and characteristics do they have? Is there a common thread among them? Your role models can be people you can talk to such as family members, or people you can gain access to. They can be famous people with whom you may not be able to have a conversation, but who you will find doing talks, interviews, YouTube videos, and may have written books talking about how they got where they are. Study them. Put them on your vision board that you will create shortly.

Perhaps you don't know anyone who has the kind of love relationship or friendships you want to have. Don't worry! Simply think about your list of what you love and like and what you dislike and find to be complete deal breakers and write the qualities your ideal partner and friends will have. **What does he/she like to do? What's most important to her? What are her values? What are his hobbies? How do your friends and partner treat you? What does your life feel like with these people in your world?** The more detail you write, the clearer the energy you're sending out. Remember: vague details, vague results. Sweatpants.

You're a role model too.

> **"One filled with joy preaches without preaching."**
> **-Mother Teresa,**
>
> *St. Teresa of Calcutta, Albanian Indian Roman Catholic nun and missionary, ultimate good deed doer and selfless woman*

As you are living, breathing and identifying your role models, remember that you are a role model as well. You might not be famous or as successful as you want to be, but you are, nonetheless, 100% a role model. You have friends, children, nieces, nephews, siblings, cousins, peers, coworkers, and acquaintances in your life. You are a human on the planet around other humans, therefore you are a role model. If you have children, you're a role model for a future generation. Much of human behavior is what was role modeled for you in your early environment. No pressure!

You learned to see the world and respond to it, in part, by the way your parents saw and responded to it. You might have changed your mind as you got older, with the addition of new information and new role models, but as a parent, your kids are learning to think, speak, and act as you do. And don't kid yourself, they don't miss a thing. They might not understand it, but they will sure as shit repeat it. Be what you want them to become, no matter how much work it is for you. Your family, friends, coworkers, and acquaintances will benefit from this as well. See the good in the world and be the good you want to see. I know I said getting rid of your negative self-talk was the work most worth doing, if you were only going to do one thing in this book. But being the good in the world you want to see is "for real" the work most worth doing. Okay, after you get rid of the negative messages. Role modeling positive self-talk, fucking awesome.

The process of identifying role models has one more purpose which is to teach you to live consciously. Live your life intentionally and with purpose. Create your life. Look for clues. There are no accidents or coincidences, but you must do the work, which sometimes is just to be fully alive and willing to participate in your destiny.

What I know for sure (to borrow Oprah's famous line) is that just one role model is enough to change a person's whole trajectory. In a life well-lived, you will have many. If you're awake, they will find you and you will know them when you feel them.

NOTES

You will stand on the shoulders of giants. Then you will sit down and have cocktails with them. Finally, you will become one of the giants.

What I ridiculously love in this chapter:

Who are my role models and why?

What kind of role model do I want to be?

Affirmation:

Every day in every way I am the best version of myself.

PART II
GET REAL

COMING UNGLUED SO YOU CAN GET UNSTUCK

"Our concern must be to live while we're alive…to release our inner selves from the spiritual death that comes with living behind a façade designed to conform to external definitions of who and what we are."
-Elizabeth Kubler-Ross

CHAPTER 8

Regain Wonder. Seeing the World Through the Eyes of a Child While Still Being Able to Drink Jack Daniels and Swear Like a Sailor

"Wonder is the heaviest element on the periodic table. Even a tiny fleck of it stops time."
Diane Ackerman,
poet, essayist and naturalist

Why do we stop believing in magic and seeing the world as a place of wonder anyway?

We live in the age of internet and cable television that provide endless amounts of information about people doing extraordinary things, so why do we ever stop believing that everything is possible for us? Why do we believe that what's possible for us is any less than what's possible for Oprah, Elon Musk, Richard Branson, Tony Robbins, or any other person who started with nothing and built an incredible life?

Maybe you don't want extraordinary. Nah. That's not it.

You just don't know how to get there.

Maybe you're too closely aligned with friends and family who are where you are, rather than following the footsteps of someone who's where you want to be. Maybe someone told you that you will never amount to much, and you believed them because they were in a position of power and trust over you.

Maybe you're so busy checking things off your proverbial lists that you've lost touch with what you like and love in favor of what you think you *should* be doing. You forget what you wanted, or you never knew in the first place.

We start powering through life and forget there's another mode. What we knew we wanted gets shoved deep inside over the years of trials and tribulations called life.

Most likely you told yourself that you needed to be a grown up and get a job. You tossed out your dream of being an actress along with your stuffed animals and started working at a job that had nothing to do with the theater. You stopped doing plays once you graduated from high school. You gave up. Maybe you gave up because you thought you weren't good enough. But you also didn't have the support to make it happen.

That's what happened to me with dance. I took private and class lessons through high school. No one other than my friends were involved, encouraging me. My mom thought it was a pipe dream. At the end of my one and only year as a classical ballet major, I decided to do the practical thing and switch to a business major. I look back on that year as a dancer more favorably than any other until I went back to study psychology because I was doing something I loved and, because of that, the world was an amazing place.

Science says the world is wondrous. And it knows.

There's a lot we don't know for sure. Science says so. For example, we can only see three dimensions (length, width, and height) when Superstring Theory scientists believe that there are ten dimensions. That means there is much more happening in the physical world than we can even see with our limited vision. Psychological research studies testify to the fact we miss much of, and sometimes major things, that happen around us. Google the

Monkey Business Illusion by Daniel J. Simon and Whodunnit (https://www.youtube.com/watch?v=ubNF9QNEQLA) to see just how oblivious we really are. We also know that we don't hear or smell nearly as well as our furry and finned counterparts in the animal kingdom. Human memory is also not as good as we think it is. We make incorrect associations when our brains file new information, make mistakes in recalling information, and we misinterpret what we file and recall because our complex brains fill in gaps, delete information, and make incorrect assumptions in the name of efficient processing and storage of large volumes of input. And, we're all biased in multiple ways which causes errors in judgment. Scientists have gone to great lengths in research to show us how feeble we really are. We aren't as good as we think we are.

We have no good reason to think we know all that's possible for ourselves or anyone else. If we don't know all that's possible, we don't know for sure if anything is impossible. And that is how you begin to live in the world of all possibilities. And the answer to the question at the beginning of this chapter is?

Why do we stop believing in magic and seeing the world as a place of wonder anyway? **Practicality.**

Practicality is the death of our sense of wonder about the world along with our belief in miracles. Practicality dealt the final blow to my dance dream. Business was practical. Reliable. And this, my friends, is how our dreams die.

Disney, the Easter Bunny and Santa, Oh My!

"Imagination is more important than knowledge."
-ALBERT EINSTEIN,
German born theoretical physicist, developer of the theory of relativity and super smart genius guy

When you were a little kid, the world seemed like a magical place. You lived as easily in the land of make-believe as you did in the real world. You didn't yet know all the limitations the world would one day place on your dreams. You believed you could be and do anything you wanted. Princess? Yes, please. You believed you could be a famous actress. You believed you could have millions of dollars, wear pretty clothes and drive fancy cars. You believed you could be an Olympic gymnast or President. Disney World, Disney movies and Disney everything served as proof that the world is magical. Disney is still very magical though slightly less so when you're a grownup paying your own way.

You most likely remember when and how you found out about Santa and the Easter Bunny. But when did we stop seeing the world as a wondrous place? You probably can't pinpoint it. Was it when you chose your college major? Maybe you were younger like middle school and high school when real world stuff shows up such as bullying, cliques, diets, bad hair days, acne and periods. Challenges and disappointments make the world seem less awesome. Whether the end of your awe was a gradual erosion or cataclysmic event, we can all return to thinking the world is stupendous and believing in a bit of magic.

How you see the world is mindset.

There is no one concrete reality. It's perspective. If you choose to see the world as totally fucking mind-blowing, you will find evidence to support that every day. If you think the world is shitty and out to get you, you will find evidence of that.

You don't have to take my word for it. Try it yourself. Just like with self-talk, what you tell yourself about the world is up to you. I live in the same world as those around me with the same climate change, devastating catastrophes, and seemingly endless problems that need fixed. I can focus on the problems and become weighted down by them like some people I know, or I can limit my intake of news about the crises and focus on news from the individuals and groups working on the solutions. Both exist and are plentiful. I live in the same town with congested traffic, northerners who move in and stay three or four months a year to escape the cold, high food prices, monopolistic resource suppliers, and I could go on and on. I could focus on what's bothersome about where I live, or I can leave early enough to deal with traffic and take time every day to notice the beauty of the absolute tropical paradise in which I live. You get to choose what you focus on. You get to choose to live a high vibe life full of wonder and possibility or a low vibe life that comes from thinking about all that's wrong and how it negatively affects you. You see, reality is in the eye of the beholder.

So how do you rewind and regain your sense of wonder?

There are many ways to get it back and not all of them involve bourbon, though bourbon does work nicely. Small steps. Here is a list of some short activities, that don't induce a hangover, and will help you regain an open, uncluttered mind, one that maybe even believes in miracles. It'll feel weird at first. Irresponsible too. If you feel silly, you're doing it right.

1. **Spend time with children.** No cell phone or distractions. Get involved in their imaginative play. Let the child be the leader, and you follow his lead. Whether it's Legos, pretend play, dress up or a field trip, get involved in the story and leave the real world behind. Read a book to a small child and observe how they immerse themselves in the story. You're studying their thoughts, feelings, and actions so you can learn from the child how to get back to being child-like but with responsibilities. This is an exercise in suspending your disbelief.
2. **Create.** Color. Crayons, colored pencils, and coloring book (adult or child) or draw your own pictures. Paint, even if you don't think you can. Finger-paint. Write a story. Let whatever wants to come out do so. No editing.

3. **Learn something new.** You don't know everything and sometimes we get stuck in the "things" we usually do, which gives us a certain expertise. What interests you that you know little about? Do you want to know more about dinosaurs but never had time to read what the earth was like when T Rex roamed? Well, now is the time to find out. Who knows, maybe you'll discover that digging for bones is your retirement gig.
4. **Read a book (or listen to one) that shifts or reminds you of your spiritual and metaphysical beliefs** such as E-Cubed by Pam Grout, May Cause Miracles or Miracles Now by Gabrielle Bernstein, The Law of Attraction by Esther and Jerry Hicks, The Hidden Messages in Water by Dr. Masaru Emoto, Proof of Heaven-A Neurosurgeon's Journey into the Afterlife by Eben Alexander, or if you like physics, read about String Theory.
5. **Walk in nature.** Bike, swim, run if you like. The key is to observe. Just be. Breathe. No electronics. Notice the sky, people, bugs, animals, flowers, sounds, scents, the breeze. Reconnect with the ecosystem around you. Regain a sense of insignificance as you are only a player in an amazing dynamic world that is so much bigger than you with so much going on. It can't possibly be a coincidence the way nature and the world works can it?
6. **Do something that scares you.** Do something that challenges what you think your limits are and scares you a little. Conquering fear even one small fear at a time shows you that you are more powerful than you give yourself credit for. If you think you can only walk a mile or two, sign up to run a 5k. If you don't think you can get through an hour of cardio fitness, take a class. If you don't think you can get through a college class, take one. If you don't think you can give a speech, do it anyway. Post it on YouTube or Facebook. You want to be a published author, start sharing your work.

7. **Shift your focus.** Rather than thinking about "what if it doesn't work out," think about what your life will be like if it does. What if you could be, do and have whatever you want? How will it feel? Other people get what they want. Why not you?
8. **Find stories of people with bigger challenges, obstacles, and limitations than you have, who are doing things that seem impossible.** Marc Zupan, a wheelchair rugby player, played in the 2004 and 2008 (gold winning) Paralympic Games and was featured in the movie Murderball. In 2012, Sister Madonna Buder completed an Ironman Triathlon at 82. Nola Ochs graduated from college at 95. Not to mention those who have pursued their dreams through physical obstacles: Stevie Wonder, Helen Keller, President Franklin D. Roosevelt and Stephen Hawking to name a few. Try reading stories on Humans of NY.
9. **Let shit go.** Let go of what caused you pain in the past, what didn't work, and what went wrong. Focus on the good in each day and what went right. Set down the weight of the world and let your shoulders and arms find their new, upright normal. Really.
10. **Play with the world.** Try stuff. Ignore what you know and do shit anyway. Surrender trying to figure everything out. Focus on what you want and let the Universe figure out how to give it to you. Prepare to be surprised. Expect miracles.
11. **Practice gratitude.** When you spend time each day, saying what you are grateful for, you're focusing on what you're grateful for, which means you'll get more of it. When you list what you appreciate, you will find so many more things than you ever realized. Once you get through the items that are a given, your kids, dog, job, husband, wife, roof over your head kind of stuff, you'll eventually have to start expanding to stuff like that the sky is the most amazing blue. By the way, gratitude also makes you feel good.

The eleven tools above are just an example of what you can do. These are all things I've personally used to remind myself that the world is magical, despite what isn't going my way on any given day. My friend Abigail lays on her patio and looks at the clouds when she needs to step out of the grind and remind herself that the world is amazing. Another of my friends swings on her kids' swing set. I sit in a chair under the bamboo in my back yard and just watch nature, which is quickly and delightfully oblivious to my presence. The birds, bugs, and squirrels happily do what they do, and I am reminded that the world is spectacular in its complex simplicity. It feels good to be insignificant and unnecessary for a few moments. The ecosystem in my yard does not ask me for anything, and I am free to just marvel at its existence. Do what resonates with you.

The true wonder in our human experience is this, however. Having been on this planet enough decades to be certain I have lived at least half my life, I can tell you what I know for sure.

You get the exact experiences you are meant to have, to become the person you are meant to be.

Some of those will be amazing, and some will be awful. They happen exactly when they're meant to and give you the raw material for the story of you. You are co-creating with a power greater than yourself. That, alone, is sufficient to evoke a sense of wonder about the world. It's easier to see that this is true the older you get, assuming you've taken a few moments to breathe and look back. If you do so, you will see that everything you've gone through was an important contributor to who you are. The lesson isn't to get stuck in any one experience, year, decade, role, or in the emotion of any of them but to let all of it show you pieces of the puzzle of you, the you that you are meant to be, so that you can do the work that you are meant to do and make the contributions you are meant to make.

You don't get answers from a book, you get clues. The answers come from life.

Life's a puzzle, and you must take a moment to put the pieces together and then reflect on the big picture. When you release the struggle and pain, the puzzle comes together, and you can see the picture clearly. There are no accidents or coincidences. Each moment, every single thing is as it's meant to be. The good, the bad, and the ugly. And it's always right on time. You're not late in getting to anything. You're right where you're meant to be. All is well, and all will be well because that's how life works. Nothing is more wonderful than that.

NOTES

Perspective is as unique as DNA.
When you change how you see the world, the world you see changes.

What I *ridiculously* love in this chapter:

What small steps will I take today:

Affirmation:

The world is magical and I am part of the magic.

CHAPTER 9

Create a Bucket List

"A man who dares waste one hour of life has not discovered the value of life."
-Charles Darwin,
English naturalist and major contributor to the science of evolution, original travel blogger

The bucket list has been given a bum rap. It's become known as this list you create at a certain ripe old age of things to do before you "kick the bucket." Good Kookaboo as my Aunt Rosalie says. Aunt Rosalie is my nana's sister. Even at 94, she's the same saucy 5'1" woman I've always known, only moving a bit slower.

Back to bucket lists. Man, do they have bucket lists all wrong!

A bucket list is a guide for living a meaningful, adventurous, life! This is how you make sure you are living to the width of your life and not just to the length of it. And if you're going to do it right, you better start while you're young. There's no such thing as too young to create a bucket list. There's no such thing as too old to create one either but, if your nine-year-old wants to create her bucket list because she sees you doing it, immediately give her a piece of paper! That's a hell yeah. She'll be better at it than you too, because she isn't going to censor her answers. She's going to think about everything she even remotely wants to do, and she's going to put it on the list. She's not going to think about whether it's possible, or too complicated, or whether she'll have the time, money, and energy to do it.

She won't consider if she has the brain power or dexterity for it either. For kids, it's simple. No filters. Do I like it? Would it be a blast to do this thing? Yeah. K. Write it down.

You could even host a bucket list party. Pairs well with rosé. Or martinis. But, then again, what doesn't? Alcohol, consumed responsibly, releases your judgment and inhibitions. It makes you unclench. It helps you to focus on yourself. You get closer to being a dreamer again.

I know every time I drink with my best friend, Lori, we plan travel adventures. Dreamers. But then we end up creating the next trips we take together. Doers. Dream it, do it.

Getting right down to business. Let's do this. Brain dump, style.

The Bucket List Exercise.

Write down 100 things you want to do, be, have, learn, and achieve before you die. Put everything on there even if you think you might not get to it. Put it on there regardless of whether or not you feel it'll take too much time or money to accomplish. Add items to the list even if you're pretty sure you'll be too afraid to do them, but you definitely want to. Also include all the things you want to do but think are impossible. I don't want you to think about "how" to make it happen right now, only that you want it to. If people will think you're batshit crazy for even thinking about doing it, add it to the list and highlight it. Hello Ironwoman. There you are, girl who writes her memoir.

This is an "everything is possible" bucket list. Write down the quick, lengthy, outlandish, fear-inducing, normal, expensive, wild, and yes, the crazy. Include the "I might see a unicorn before I accomplish x" things.

The intentional life.

The reason creating a bucket list is important is that it puts you in the mental zone of creating your life while telling your inner critic and practical brain to shush. Your intentional dreamer takes the wheel. You probably need practice shifting gears to a feeling of powerful badass. Destination: to create your life rather than your life happening to you and dealing with whatever comes. Also, you may be so practical that you're ignoring the magnitude of all that we don't know about the world and all that we do know about manifesting.

If you do a two second Google search, you can find an endless number of ordinary people doing extraordinary things such as Yuichiro Miura, who climbed Mt Everest at 70, 75 and most recently at 80 years old, or Amy Purdy who is a double amputee snowboarder. It's not a matter of whether something is possible or not, everything is possible. What you need to ask yourself is, how badly do I want to do it?

> *"The only thing you are governed by is how badly you want something, everything else is an excuse."*

This is one of my favorite mantras. I created it to remind myself that nothing is impossible. And to catch myself when I fall into the old habit of focusing on why I can't do something. I've had people argue with me about the truth of this mantra but turns out they were completely snowed by their excuses. I mean, if you're going to create excuses as to why you're not doing something, make them so good that even you believe they're true.

We also get confused about the order of things. When I have more time, I'll take ballroom dance lessons or write the book. The proper order is to begin the classes or the manuscript. Feel the energy that comes from focusing on what makes you happy. More time, energy and money for those things magically appears. Everything else in your life goes better too.

Seeing what sticks.

Creating a bucket list is sort of like throwing spaghetti at the wall to see what sticks. Some of you will work through the bucket list like it's your job, adding things to it as you cross other things off. Most will accomplish a few things here and there. If you have 100 things on your bucket list, you're more like to achieve some of them than if you have no bucket list or a bucket list of five things. A bucket list is a way to be clear about what you want to do, be real about what and who will take the journey with you (and who won't), and it's a starting point to accomplish stuff. Maybe a long bucket list means a long, happy, adventurous life. Don't get me wrong, it's also okay to have a long, simple life as well. Maybe your bucket list is the 100 (or 10,000) books you want to read. Maybe your bucket list is the 100 conversations you want to have. Maybe it's places you want to visit or foods you want to eat. A traditional bucket list contains a variety of activities but yours need not. Maybe you have multiple bucket lists. What matters is that whatever is on your bucket list puts meaning into your life. Meaning and well-being equal happiness.

"I don't want to get to the end of my life and find out I have lived just the length of it. I want to have lived the width of it as well."
-Diane Ackerman
poet, essayist and naturalist

Many of the things on my bucket list, which is currently at 70 items, are very identifiable and will either be checked off the list or not. Your bucket list is fluid, meaning if you no longer want to do something, you can remove it from the list and put something else in its place. Having a bucket list should never feel oppressive like all those college classes you have to take to get your degree (hello, history 101) but don't want to. Your bucket list is an adventure. If you don't want to do something, don't put it on the list.

Here are some examples from my list, which I created a few years ago: #3 Become fluent in French, #7 visit Puerto Rico, #12 See humpback whales (achieved July 2018, Monterrey, CA!) and #44 Own an Oscar de la Renta ball gown and #50 Have an occasion to wear the ball gown in #44. I will clearly know when I have achieved those things and can cross them off the list. Notice I didn't say "if". I didn't give myself that out. I'm sure I want those things because I've been dreaming of them for years.

Making it happen.

Seeing humpback whales didn't happen by accident. I chose it. I wanted to see them in Monterrey, California, as my top pick of what to do on our vacation out west in the summer of 2018. I got the buy-in of my travel mates. I know sightseers regularly see humpback whales there as well as gray whales and sometimes blue whale too. We'd only seen orcas when we went whale watching in Monterrey on a family vacation in 2006. I also got seasick on that 2006 whale watching excursion so this time I meditated the night before, during the night, and in the morning, during which I visualized myself feeling great on the boat, energetic even, and not the least bit nauseous. I envisioned seeing humpback whales and being completely awestruck at their magnificence.

We got on the boat around 9am that morning, I took deep breaths and focused on calm mind and stomach. The trip was beyond amazing. I was perfectly fine even though there were people who were seasick all around me. The whales showed up closer to shore than they usually do, so we only had to travel out for one hour before we found a magnificent feeding display that lasted the whole duration of our whale watch tour. There were so many lunges and a spectacular breech very close to our boat. It was better than I could have ever imagined, and I felt perfectly fine the whole time, even though the Pacific was rough, as usual. The weather, also perfect.

Never doubt that you are more in control of your experience of life than you imagined.

If it's on the list, I plan to accomplish it, even the scary and intimidating ones like #16 Do a Ted Talk and #35 Run a marathon. Those will both take a great deal of preparation and carry the possibility that I might vomit or die in the middle of them. Both of those things are seriously intimidating to me at this moment. I have never run a 5k without having to walk for a few minutes here and there, and I can do an hour of cardio without being overly taxed right now. And I've only recently begun putting myself out there as a speaker.

Skip the subjective.

I started out having a few items on the list that were more subjective such as, #1 Be a well-respected writer and #24 Help kids in the foster care system in a bigger way (than I'm currently doing as a Guardian ad Litem volunteer). Those and a few others had some arbitrary success metric that I assumed I'd recognize when I had achieved it. They weren't completely vague but not binary like the first bucket list items I mentioned. I ended up revising them to be very clear: achieved or not achieved yet because it's no fun to have to say (in progress) next to all your items or to be unclear when you might cross them off the list. It turns out that crossing things off your list because you've achieved them, is really fun! Almost as much fun as doing the thing! I don't recommend having vague items on your list. You want most of your items to be either clearly "did it" or "not yet".

Some of the items on your list may require a lot of preparation, but some of them will take either a moderate amount or not much effort at all. Several of my items could be crossed off with a couple days visit to LA and to NYC such as a visit to the Met Costume Institute (#43) (went there in January 2019 but found out you can't see it because it's not open to the public), see a Broadway show on Broadway (#52), and to visit the cemeteries, Forest Lawn and Forever Hollywood, where my favorite movie icons are buried (#41). Several others could be crossed off the list with $50,000 of disposable income that I can spend on vintage or current fashion such as the De La Renta ball gown (#44), owning a Gianni Versace original anything (#46), a pair of Manolo Blahnik shoes (got them in March 2019!) (#51), and a classic Chanel suit (#45). Still others require opportunity to knock. Yes, I'm planning on it, preparing for it, and visualizing it but it's not entirely up to me like #20, 21, and 22 which are meeting Oprah Winfrey, Tony Robbins, and doing projects with both that help millions of people.

Do the damn thing!

A bucket list is simply what you want to accomplish that gives your life meaning and adventure. It keeps you from wandering unless you want to wander. Some are easy, some are more difficult. Some are inexpensive or free, and some require savings or a windfall of unneeded cash. Some items require planning and preparation while others need none. Whatever you put on your list is what you plan to accomplish because it will make you feel good to do it. You've conquered a fear or an extensive regimen (as in training for a marathon) to get there. Others are where opportunity meets intention. Some tasks might be in progress because they can't be completed in a day or week like becoming fluent in French (#4), which I work on for a few minutes each week when I read social media posts in French.

You don't have to list them in the order that you plan to accomplish the items: just get everything on the list.

It's perfectly acceptable to do number 62 before you do number one. They don't have to be prioritized or classified: fashion, travel, free, expensive, or anything else but of course you can organize them and prioritize them if you want to.

Yes to this but fuck that.

And yes! Absolutely you can choose to eliminate something from the list if you decide you no longer want to do that thing. I used to have learning to scuba dive on my list, but I neither accomplished it nor really feel like I want to do it. If I change my mind about it later, I will put it back on the list. I have consciously decided, however that I like to be near the water, not in it. I even occasionally like to be on it (on a cruise ship) but not in it. I've snorkeled and decided that was enough. My goal of learning to swim under water without holding my nose (#32) will be accomplished in a swimming pool. I have also added some things to my list that weren't there before like (#26) writing a memoir and learning to speak a little Russian (#40). There are quite a few visitors to St Petersburg Florida, where I live, that speak Russian. I hear it in stores several times a year. I like the way it sounds and the complexity of it. The fact that I studied romance languages, which are so different than Russian also makes learning Russian exciting. So, it's on the list. It's also a do much later item. I've accomplished things that used to be on the list such as becoming a certified guardian ad litem volunteer, owning a Mercedes Benz (though I don't have one now and would like another one!), and visiting Paris.

I've realized that I prefer to leave items on the list but cross them off when I achieve them because then the list is like a working documentary of my adventurous life.

Now you get the methodology of the Bucket List, how to create one, and why it's a really important to do it now rather than later. For those of you who are curious as to the items I haven't mentioned here, I have included my complete bucket list, at this moment in time, in the back of the book. The list of things I want to accomplish, is, as I've stated, a living document. Yours will be too. It's your list for a life well-lived, whatever that is for you.

Journalist and *Fear and Loathing in Las Vegas* author, Hunter S. Thompson summarized how I feel about life and death quite nicely:

"Life should not be a journey to the grave with the intention of arriving safely in a pretty and well-preserved body, but rather to skid in broadside in a cloud of smoke, thoroughly used up, totally worn out, and loudly proclaiming 'Wow! What a ride!'"

Your bucket list is your road map to ensure just this sort of journey or whatever journey you want to have is an intentional one. No wandering, unless your goal is, specifically and clearly, to wander. If you need motivation, think about what you will regret if you don't do it. How will you feel if you live a life ruled by fear rather than fun? A life of so-so rather than spectacular? Don't leave what matters most to you, your very awesome life, up to chance. Grab it by the man parts while twirling your lasso high in the air. Let's go ladies!

NOTES

Adventure. Rest. Repeat

What I *ridiculously* love in this chapter:

Hell Yeah! Bucket List Items:

Affirmation:

I am living my life as one big joyous adventure.

CHAPTER 10

Rewrite Your Story. Be Your Own Fucking Fairy Godmother and Buy Your Own Shoes and Dress

"Oh, it's a beautiful dress! Did you ever see such a beautiful dress? And look! Glass slippers. Why, it's like a dream. A wonderful dream come true."
-Cinderella,
dreamer who went after her dream and married a prince despite having an evil stepmother and sisters

Don't you just wish your fairy godmother would show the fuck up already? I've wanted mine to come to my rescue so many times. I prayed for her to appear when my mom could only afford two pairs of Gloria Vanderbilt jeans that we found on sale as I was going into seventh grade, circa 1979. Don't get me wrong, I was grateful for those two pair of jeans! I was happy to have them. I chose them over three pair of non-designer jeans. I wanted to have diversity in my designers though. I correctly predicted that I would be bullied for having only Gloria Vanderbilt jeans. No matter how hard I prayed, no fairy came to my rescue.

She also didn't show up when I needed a prom dress in high school. And unlike Molly Ringwald's character in Pretty in Pink, I couldn't just sew bits of dresses together to make something fantastic. Don't cry for me, Argentina! I didn't get asked to my high school proms anyway.

I realized at some point that I'm holding the wand. I am the fairy godmother I've been wishing for. If I want it, I can get it.

Why do you get to rewrite your story? Because you are your own fairy godmother, too. You want the fairy tale? Create it. You're so much more powerful than you know. It turns out that, like Dorothy, you've had it all along. And it doesn't even matter that you didn't know it before. What matters is that you know it now.

Where's my wand?

How is it possible to choose your future story? Why should you believe you, your life, love, and work can be better than it ever has been?

You're not a kid anymore, so you don't believe in fairy tales. The past is what you know best. What's happened so far in your life is what your subconscious is familiar with. It's a short leap to conclude that your future will be more of the same. It's easier for your mind to live strong in what you've experienced; it's much harder to envision what you haven't.

But here's two reasons why this is a habit you want to break right now: (1) Fairy tales come true for some people. Look at Chelsea Handler, Jim Carrey, Leighton Meester, Leonardo DiCaprio, Shania Twain, Sarah Jessica Parker or any of thousands of other people living their dream come true, who started with nothing more than a dream or at least a gut feeling they were willing to follow. (2) The past does not predict the future. No two situations are exactly the same, and you are not the same from one day to the next. You learn new information that changes the way you see the world. Subtle shifts accumulate over time. If the variables change even a little bit, the outcome does too. That said, you may be playing out similar patterns of thought, emotion, and behavior that are not serving your goals, dreams, and ambition. All of that can be changed.

When I work with clients, I always figure out what motivates them and what their beliefs are. The women and men who reach out to me reliably document their faith and a belief in something much greater than themselves, regardless of whether they call it God, the Universe, the Goddess, or something else. Yet so much of what they say after the proclamation of faith speaks of fear. It's impossible to have faith and fear in a single moment. Faith, defined by Merriam-Webster, "is a belief, trust in and loyalty to God" or, "a firm belief in something for which there is no proof." Fear is born of uncertainty, a lack of trust. You have one or the other. The essence of faith is the absence of fear. Awareness of this dichotomy is powerful. It returns us in the direction of home. Fear can show up on your doorstep with bags in hand, prepared to stay awhile, but you can choose not to open the door. You can lean into your faith, get cozy with it, rely on it. Hold onto it so tightly it can't breathe. Then let it wrap its gentle, faithful arms around you, reassuringly.

Faith vs. unshakeable faith.

One of the difficulties, however, of relying on faith, is that you feel it has let you down before. You were taught to have faith as a little child in Sunday church services. Yet bad stuff happened. It might let you down again.

They did not teach you to have unshakeable faith and may have simultaneously and confusingly been teaching you fear. And you did not have a clear vision of what you want. Being a novice at faith and the skills that generate clarity are what failed you in the past, not faith itself. This is what caused you to open the door, through which fear has charged in and sometimes stayed for a very long time. When you are living with fear, you are eating, sleeping, and breathing what you don't want. Energetically, you draw that which you focus on to you. You didn't even know you were doing it. More of what you fear shows up over time because you have focused on it, and mistakenly, you think your connection to God is broken. You think your faith isn't working, but you don't realize you abandoned it and let fear slither into its place.

Light bulb moment.

Focus on what you do not want, get more of that. Focus on what you do want, get more of that.

Like unto itself is drawn. It's so stated in the Law of Attraction. It's energetic. I've experimented with it. I'm telling you right now, that little epiphany is at the base of the mountain you will climb to change your life. The better at it you get, the more the mountain becomes a hill, then an ant hill, then just a lovely, soft green meadow of ease and comfort.

It's not your fault that you focus on what your bank account doesn't have in it: enough money to pay all your bills, buy the bag, or take the trip. You focus on what you don't have like someone to come in and clean your house so you can do more of what you want. Your brain is wired to focus on the *absence* of what you *don't* want. This is still focusing on what you don't want, giving it precious energy and drawing it near. We are biologically biased to seek pleasure and avoid pain. We have an instinctual aversion to negativity. The mistake lies in our behavior and what we do with these biological tendencies. We focus on what we don't want any more of. It's actually much easier to focus on what we do want but we have to change a sometimes decades old habit to get there.

News and media are focused on making you fear all that you lack, some of which you didn't even know existed until you saw the ad for it or a show about it. They want you to feel negative emotions about what you don't have so you'll spend money you don't have to get their supposed antidote.

You can't manifest the absence of something, only the presence of something. You will catch yourself a hundred times a day having a thought that is worry, doubt, or fear that you must immediately halt and replace with thoughts of what you do want and how happy you will feel when you have it. It's a mental exercise. Just like stopping the shit talking you do to yourself, banishing fear and replacing it with faith, takes time and practice. You will spend a lot of time and energy redirecting your thoughts which behave like a two-year-old. Your brain won't be in the terrible twos for long though if you do the work. Pretty soon you'll be good at holding up that mental stop sign and shifting to a Woodstock-style lovefest, minus the weed and port-a- potties.

Clairvoyance.

Clear vision, knowing exactly what you want or at least what you want to feel more of in your life, partnered with the belief that you can have it, are what creates the life you love. The very first thing we did in chapter one, is to identify what you love and like and what you tolerate, dislike and what are your absolute deal breakers. Now you can focus on loves and likes and get more of those. You can set boundaries that limit or eliminate everything other than likes, loves and tolerates and feel good, not guilty, doing it because this is what creates a life you love. A life of everyday joy. This is what God wants for you. I am certain that God is disappointed that we have lost our way; that we've wandered into a place where we focus so much on our problems and so little on our happiness. I am certain God wants us to choose faith. In fact, I'm pretty sure God is good with you using the F word and telling fear to just fuck the fuck off.

What you think, feel, and do in the future is based on decisions you are currently making. You can decide that you've "checked all the boxes and things didn't work out the way they were supposed to," that "everything always turns to shit," or that "the good never lasts." If that's what you focus on and believe, it's surely what you will get. A life of checked boxes and no hope.

Part of writing the story of your future life is deciding it will be exactly what you want it to be. That is not to say you won't have obstacles, challenges, and issues here and there. You will. This isn't a bad thing. You are a problem solver, and you'll simply focus on the solutions as things come up.

Why will things come up if you are now focused on what you want, and it doesn't include issues, problems, or challenges?

Great question. I was hoping you'd ask.

Partly because you were previously, before you fully engaged in this book, holding thoughts of fear and lack. Therefore, you have spent energy drawing a certain amount of what you feared to you. However, you are now going to spend less time doing that. You are paving the way for a future that includes less and less problems, issues, and challenges. Problems encourage creativity, however. Issues build our resourcefulness. They teach us and remind us who we are. You've heard the saying, "that which doesn't kill you only makes you stronger." We don't really want a complete absence of issues for therein lies our strength.

Get what you want.

You can think and feel yourself thin, healthy, pain-free, problem-free, wealthy, joyful, and anything else you want by focusing on those things. You will exercise your mental muscles to control your thoughts and hold thoughts of how you want to look and feel. Focus on how you want your life to be. Shift your focus from what's wrong or what could go wrong to thoughts of what could go right.

This is an exercise you can do sitting still and in ten minutes a day, as well as whenever your thoughts wander to the dark side. You will pull them back to the light. Prayers like "show me," "use me," "please and thank you," and "more joy please" are enough. If you do not know exactly what you want other than joy, these prayers will set in motion signs from the big U or big G that will shed light on your purpose and your path. Be deliberate in asking and believe that it will come to you. Because you are going to get the hell out of the way and allow it to do so.

Channeling Mr. or Ms. Right.

Be very clear, be emotionally involved in every detail, write every detail and use all of your senses describing your Mr. or Ms. Right so that you will know him or her when you meet. You will know him because you manifested him. If you're describing your ideal partner, name her, describe what she looks like, smells like, how he dresses, what she does, how much money he makes, what her parents and friends are like, what activities he does, how she feels about children, what kind of dad he is or will be, how she treats you and what she says to you. Write why you feel elated at the sight of him. Write why, thirty years later, you will still look forward to seeing her every day. Refer to your relationship role models if you have them. What does he do that you want in your relationships? As always, be careful not to include details of what you do not want. Don't write the absence of negative things: "he doesn't cheat on me." Write in the absolute positive, "she is 100% faithful and devoted to me, my happiness, and our happiness."

Work that sets your soul on fire.

If you are writing about a job you want or an entrepreneurial endeavor, use the same process. Describe your employers, employees, coworkers, business partners, associates, the work you do, and how you feel doing the work. Describe how you feel every day in your work environment. Do you work in an office or from home? If you are an entrepreneur, describe your products or services; describe your amazing clients and what they say about your products or services. How do you help them? What problem do you solve for them? Describe why you do what you do. Describe very clearly how much money you make each week, month, and year. Be sure to include the amount you need so that you can live abundantly so that you're able to spend, save, invest, and donate as much as you'd like each year. Describe how you will spend the money and how you will feel, easily being able to spend this money and do more of what you love. Describe whom you will donate money to, why, and what it means to you to donate it to your chosen causes. Describe the impact your money, joy, and happiness will have on those closest to you. It is impossible to use too much detail. It's perfectly acceptable to begin with how you want to feel and fill in more and more details as signs begin to show themselves. Put in as much detail as you can right now and fill it in as you go if need be.

La Famiglia.

Describe relationships with your children, your family, and your friends as you want them to be and not as they are. What are they like, what do they do with you and for you? Talk about how your friends lift you up. Talk about how your friends always have your back and you have theirs, no matter what. Who's the Gail to your Oprah? Who are the Samantha, Charlotte and Miranda to your Carrie Bradshaw? Talk about how your kids are really kind humans who are going to change the world (and hopefully help us fix its problems).

Details, details and more details.

Describe pets you'd like to have. Where (in the world) will you live and visit? Describe your house. How does your house feel, what's in it? Where is it located? What kind of car do you have? What do you do with your free time? Do you volunteer? Garden? Raise orchids? Write a novel? Learn to play the piano? Refer to your bucket list to make sure you are capturing things you want to do and learn. This, too, is a living document and can be changed. My story of my present and future life changes a little here and there, but it mostly has been set because I figured out years ago what my passion and purpose are, and I spend my days doing it. I do not teach anything I have not personally done, even the science-based principles of happiness and success.

You can create all the facets of your life simultaneously, and it always begins with a long, clear declaration of what you want. It begins with a vision in your head of a happy, radiant, joyful you. You smile so often people wonder what you're up to. People tell you that you look happy, vibrant and younger, the magic Y word. People will tell you how good you look, not because you have found some beauty product that works like magic, but because there is a light that radiates out from your fulfilled soul and overflowing heart. Warning: You may even start hugging people more often, including people you don't know. It comes with the shift in energy. You will become more protective of your state and not let in information and people that bring you down.

I wish we could all have a fairy godmother that magically appears and makes us the belle of the ball with whom Prince Charming falls madly in love, and we live happily ever after. I certainly always hoped one would appear and whisk me out of a childhood I had to survive.

I wish I could be your fairy godmother and that my passion for your happiness would suffice to create it for you. But I realized that maybe I could teach you to be your own and that it's not only enough, but that it's fucking awesome and way better than relying on me or some pudgy, little, wand-waving winged woman. You have you for the rest of your days.

So, here's your chance to change the ending from what you thought it would be to what you want it to be. Or maybe you didn't even think about what it would be. Either way, now you will *consciously* write it for the first time. Pretend you're writing a paper for school. Be a kid again. Write what your life is going to look, smell, taste, feel, and sound like from now on. Talk about what you do, who you are, what you love about yourself, what you've accomplished, and why you're proud of yourself. What gives your life meaning? Talk about everything that is even somewhat significant in this life. Do you reconcile with estranged family or find your birth parents? Describe how you got here to this amazing life you crazy love. Talk about where you started and the steps you took to get from lackluster to lovely life. Pay homage to those who helped you along the way. No one does it alone and gratitude creates happiness. It's like adding a sprinkle of pixie dust to the story.

"Your brain is your bitch."

-Jen Sincero

NY Times bestselling nonfiction author who is stand-up comedian funny which makes my job so much harder but makes her a most worthwhile mentor for whom I am profoundly grateful

---

Why write it out? Why so much detail?

It puts you in the scene. You can get the six-sensory experience that engages as many brain regions as possible. You want your brain to believe it's in that reality and to begin to make subconscious decisions accordingly. You want your brain to create thoughts, which invoke emotions, and those thoughts and emotions in turn, govern your future actions toward this new reality. You won't even realize it's happening. But you must write it out in detail and spend time rereading it daily until you can flip a switch and mentally experience it for a few minutes every day. In the next chapter we'll add visual cues that will make you daydream about your new life for a few minutes each day. You want your triggers to easily transport you. And you want to become so familiar with it, laser focused and automatic, that your brain starts subliminally scanning your environment for anything that fits in that reality such as the house, the man, and the opportunities that create the life you love. This is what's really happening when people talk about manifesting- getting super clear about what you want, laser focusing your brain and readying yourself to receive it by shifting your beliefs and energy. There's science behind the woo-woo of manifestation, and as I said before, it's really easy to trick your brain. So do it.

Make your story fairy-tale worthy. Put it on pretty paper. Add glitter.

There's no such thing as a dream too big and nor are there any steps too small. Dream big, take a step.

Dreams without action are just wishes. Wishes weren't good enough for Cinderella, and they definitely aren't good enough for you. Feel the exhilaration of being your own fairy godmother. *It's wand-waving time.* Go you!

NOTES

My future story begins today.

What I ridiculously love in this chapter:

Where does my story begin?

Affirmation:

I am co-creating my life. I open the doors and windows to opportunities and happily pursue them.

CHAPTER 11

From Vision Board to Ouija Board: Let the Magic Begin With Visual Cues

"Everyone wants some magical solution for their problems yet everyone refuses to believe in magic."
Mad Hatter,
From <u>*Alice in Wonderland*</u> *by Lewis Carroll*

Get ready to let your inner creative off the chain. Pretty chain, you know, with diamonds and other sparkly gems. But we're unleashing you. Your vision board is a total creative expression of your dreams and goals and must be specific yet representative of all you desire. For example, if you want a black Mercedes sedan, print a picture of the exact one and put that on your board. If you want to meet Tony Robbins put his picture on there. You may want your ideal house, but you've not yet found it; put images that represent your ideal, such as a house on the water in the style you love. If you want to get a college degree, put the college logo and a picture of the diploma on your board.

You may be wondering why you need a vision board. You're already journaling like a mad scientist and doing enough homework to earn you a college degree, so why a vision board too? And you probably have some scary memory of playing with a Ouija board as a kid, even though your parents told you not to. I'm going to start off by telling you why I want you to take the time, spend the money on a stack of magazines, glitter, and pretty paper, or whatever makes you feel happy, and do the work to create your vision board.

Why do I need a vision board? Snort. I don't have time to cut and pin pictures.

Here's the reason.

Vision boards are energy. They are vivid, visual reminders of your dreams and goals. A vision board illustrates the ideal life story you wrote in the last chapter. Your story and your vision board should be in alignment.

You might not have time to read your ideal life story every day, especially if you've made it really detailed and sensory, and it ends up being six or ten pages long. Do read it at least once a week but a vision board, placed where you can see it every day, has the effect of being a ten second reminder. A vision board really keeps you focused at a glance on where and who you want to be and on what you want to do and have. Quickly focus and refocus on what you want.

If you're focused every minute on who you want to be, how you want to feel, what you want to do and have, you won't have the mental space for thoughts about why it won't work or how that only happens for a lucky few. You want to see you and your goals everywhere. This is the immersion technique. Immersion in anything produces quick results. Like magic.

Stalk your goals.

What you want will have no choice but to come to you because it's all you think about. You're sending out super clear, uncomplicated messages to the Universe about what you want and who you are. When you look at pictures, including pictures of words, it makes it easier to feel yourself as that woman, in those places, in that car, with that Chanel bag, traveling with your family and Mr. or Ms. Right. Seeing it this way makes it easier to visualize yourself in that life before you have it. Without the visual cues, it's much harder to imagine this amazing new life, given that you've never had it and you're not there yet. Let yourself daydream on these images for even just five minutes a day. See it. Feel it. Smell the salt air on the balcony of your beach house. See people walking on the beach below you, wishing they were you. Look down and see the beautiful flowy dress and amazing shoes you're wearing. Look off to the side and see your man or woman walking through the door to the balcony with two glasses of your favorite bubbly.

Whatever you want to be, do, and have, picture it. Meditate on it. Daydream about it. And surround yourself with pictures of it.

Let yourself feel the energy of it. It's not magic. It's physics.

Law of Attraction. Like unto itself is drawn. You get what you focus on. So, focus on what you really want. No dream or goal is too big or too small. It's enough that you want it.

Post-It Notes, Index Cards, and Tattoos, Oh My.

Just kidding about the tattoos. Unless you like tattoos, in which case, one that's a positive reminder of who you are might be a hell yeah! My daughter, who also battles anxiety, has a tattoo on the inside of her arm that says, "It's all okay," because it is. She has a reminder that's always where she can see it. The good news about tattoos: your visual reminder is always with you. The bad part is that you might change your motto in time, but the tattoo is permanent.

Post-it notes and index cards comfortably fit in a purse or wallet, in the console of your car and can be stuck to your refrigerator or bathroom mirror and easily pinned to a vision board. You may have more than one mantra, as I do. You may have different quotes that inspire you. You might have affirmations you want to recite daily as well. You want these all around you.

Flip your sign.

You can make index cards so you can "flip your sign." Flip your sign is an exercise I created where you write how you feel on one side of the card and the feeling you want to replace it with on the other. For example, I have a sign that says "worried" on one side and "calm" on the other. I have another that says "perplexed" on one side and "certain" on the back of it, as well as one that says, "tired" on one side and "energetic" on the other. When I feel one way but want to feel the other way, I flip my sign. It's a simple way to change your focus, and as I've already stated, it's remarkably easy to trick your brain. Start by setting your intention and use a visual cue.

Cheesy but cheesy is good.

Write the word "smile" on a sticky note and put it on your bathroom mirror. You can also write it on a cocktail napkin and tape it up there; use whatever you have. Smiling at yourself is a great way to start your day. The self-love changes your brain chemistry. Seeing a note that says "I love you" on the mirror can turn a bad mood to a good one, not only for you but for others in the house as well.

Get your refrigerator in on it.

Next, I want you to find pictures of you, times, and places when you were happy. Put them on your refrigerator. Make a collage. Keep yourself confronted with evidence that you've had good days and happy times. You will smile when you see them, and then hello happy feelings. You get to experience the good times all over again. Seeing them may even inspire you to get back to doing more things you really enjoy. When you habituate to those pictures in a few weeks or so, change them out, and put up new ones of good times in your life.

She may have gone sign crazy.

Have multiple kinds of visual cues. These days you can easily purchase signs, coffee cups, and T-shirts that remind you of your fabulousness or the fact that life is good. My favorites are my coffee mug that says, "Good morning, Gorgeous" and my other one that says "Happy" on one side and "<3 Oprah" on the back!

There are signs in my bathroom (Happiness Never Goes Out of Style, Focus on the Good) and in my office (Be Bold, Believe You Can and You're Halfway There, Do What Makes You Happy). It's important to note that you will grow accustomed to them so you will need to change them out or at least rotate them to a different location from time to time, or your eyes will see them, but you won't consciously acknowledge the message.

The screensaver on my phone says *NY Times* Bestseller.

The big sign: vision boards

Because size matters. Let's go big. It's time to create a vision board with pictures and words. You can create a vision journal or scrapbook as well. You can get magazines and cut out images or words or print them from the internet. The key to having a vision board is to have it where you see it daily. I created a vision scrapbook in the past that I flipped through often, but for the last four years, I've had a poster-sized cork board that is on the wall near my bed. It's the first thing I see when I get up in the morning and the last visual I see when I go to bed. In my opinion this works better than having a scrapbook that you have to open. I believe the physical vision board also works better than creating it on Pinterest. You don't want to have to think about it or take to many steps to see your vision board. Easier (and bigger) is better. But please do what works best for you. Abigail has a physical vision board like I do but my client Kate has hers in an app on her phone and took a snap of it and made it her screensaver.

My vision board has my mood mantra "Bright, Cheery, Happy" at the top in bold, colorful letters. It's a daily reminder of how I want to feel each day. Intention. It has a picture of me with my family in the center of it, carefully placed to reflect their place in my life. I have the words, "Thrive Every Day" because that also sums up how I want each day to go. My vision board boasts the words, "rich," "fitness," "change agent," "the age-free life," and "energy*balance*joy." There are pictures of the house I want, the car I want, and the places I want to visit and write from along with mantras to support me getting those things. There is also a picture of Oprah and one of Tony Robbins with the saying "my mentors become my friends." Your vision board needs to describe how you want to feel, what you want to do, who is with you on the journey, who's at the destination, and what your life looks like.

Don't worry about making it too grand or thinking it's unrealistic or impractical. Do include long and short-term goals. Let it be downright magical. If you want Chanel purses, put them on your vision board. If you want to go to Greece, put pictures of Greece on there. If you want to be an entrepreneur put words and pictures on there that describe your office and what you do. If you want a new pair of shoes, put them on there.

The vision board needs to affirm where you are going and how it looks and feels. Multisensory and crystal clear. Remember vague goals, mantras, affirmations, and pictures produce vague results. Sweatpants. Be clear. You've already described this in your writing of your future story, but now you're supporting what you want further by using pictures and words on a board rather than in narrative form. Vision boards are quick yet sometimes very intricate snapshots of what you want. You want to have reminders everywhere. Varied reminders help get more parts of your brain on board with where you're headed. They prevent you from mentally, emotionally, and spiritually slipping backwards into all the reasons you won't get it by keeping you focused on what you want.

But how does it make you feel?

You should smile and feel happy when you look at your vision board. You should feel energized and inspired. If you feel "Meh," revise it. This is not a place to play it safe. If you're being conservative, practical, or critical and judgy, you're doing it wrong. And we know you want to get an A+, overachiever.

Let yourself go. I realize this may take time and practice because we're used to limiting our world to what we think is possible for us. But now we know that's hogwash. The world is wonderful and amazing and just about any damn thing is possible if you really, really want it.

Vision board to Ouija board.

Not the creepy kind of Ouija board. Imagine if you had a nice one with a genie waiting to grant your wishes. That said, energy matters. When you create a board that's super inspiring you may be surprised how fast your dreams come true. I have watched Abigail put pictures on her vision board many times and, before the glue fully dries, what she wants has shown up. I sometimes ask her if I can put stuff I want on her board because hers seems to work super fast. But don't worry if you don't manifest what you want that quickly. Don't give up and don't quit believing in the process or yourself. The only person who doesn't get what she wants is the woman who gives up or never starts. You win if you just don't quit.

As you receive, revise.

When you begin to manifest what you have on your vision board, revise it. There will be static goals and ongoing ones. For example, I had a static goal of being a *Huffington Post* writer. I wanted to be published there, but I knew from the start that I wouldn't want to do that forever. I used to have a picture of the *Huffington Post* logo on my vision board with the words *Huffington Post* blogger. I left it on there for about a year after I achieved the goal just to make sure it stuck. After a year, I took the logo off and added a picture of the *O* Magazine logo. I decided I wanted to write for *O* Magazine. On to the next exciting opportunity! And if anyone is reading this with connections to *Vogue*, *In Style*, or *Harper's Bazaar*, I'd love to write for those! If you want it, ask for it. Put it out there.

How you want to feel is an ongoing goal. I want to be bright, cheery, happy every day for the rest of my life. I'm realistic that there will be days where I will face challenges, feel stressed, or possibly even be depressed and anxious, but "Bright, Cheery, Happy" is always my target and the home base to which I return. Same for "Thrive Every Day". When will I ever not want to thrive? Also true for "age-free life." Those are ongoing.

When you think of new things you want, put them up there. Change your mind? Change your board. It's that simple. Much in life is complicated. Your vision board shouldn't be.

Have fun with this process. Make it as plain or as pretty as you want as long as what you want is clear. Have a glass a wine or host a vision board party. Enjoy it. Know that you are actively creating something that will bring you joy and happiness.

You're not passively accepting some ordinary life. You are meant to be extraordinary and now you've grabbed the Universe by the horns and you're co-creating with it.

This is how we do it. The Universe has been waiting for you.

You want more. You're meant to do, have and be more. No apologies. Be fully you.

NOTES

If a picture is worth a thousand words, your vision board is worth a million.

What I ridiculously love in this chapter:

My personal motto:

I will do my vision board beginning on:

How I feel when I look at my dreams and mottos?

Affirmation:

I see my life as I want it to be. I see it; I create it. I live it. I love it.

PART III
GET GOING

PROGRESS, NOT PERFECTION

"The 'C' students run the world."
-Harry S. Truman

CHAPTER 12

Avoid the Frying Pan. Tuning in to Your Intuition Because You Hate Cast Iron

> *"I feel there are two people inside me- me and my intuition. If I go against her, she'll screw me every time, and if I follow her, we get along quite nicely."*
> **-Kim Basinger,**
> **American actress**

Merriam says that **intuition** is "the power or faculty of attaining to direct knowledge or cognition without evident rational thought and inference; immediate apprehension or cognition." My nana, a 5'1" saucy, superstition-spouting Sicilian American, referred to intuition as **signs** (a motion or gesture by which a thought is expressed or a command or wish made known). Others call it **vibes** (**Merriam on vibrations:** a characteristic emanation, aura, or spirit that infuses or vitalizes someone or something and that can be instinctively sensed or experienced —often used in plural) and **instinct** (Gal Pal M again: a largely inheritable and unalterable tendency of an organism to make a complex and specific response to environmental stimuli without involving reason; behavior that is mediated by reactions below the conscious level).

Is intuition the same as being psychic? Not in my opinion. Or Merriam's (sensitive to nonphysical or supernatural forces and influences: marked by extraordinary or mysterious sensitivity, perception, or understanding). While some authors blur the lines between intuition and psychic or mediumship abilities, I do not. I believe each one of us has intuition at our disposal. I do not believe we all have extraordinary sensitivity to supernatural forces. We do not all know the future before it happens nor do we all see dead people.

Regardless of what we call it, when I have followed my intuition, stuff has gone better. I have really good intuition for a two reasons: (1) Because I say I do (you get what you focus on) and (2) Because I have paid attention to it since I was a little kid, so I've exercised it and developed it like a muscle. I can tell it's real because I'm old enough to have lots of outcomes to compare of when I have followed my intuition versus a few times when I didn't (but wish I had). When I trust my vibes, life is easier and when I've ignored them or acted indifferently, I've learned "lessons." Does everyone have intuition? I get this question almost as often as I get asked if we all have a purpose. Everyone has a purpose and intuition. Intuition is the internal guidance that leads you to your purpose, helps you follow your heart, and keeps you on your path- or tells you that you're off it. It also helps keep you safe. Have you ever had a feeling that something bad is about to happen or gotten a bad vibe around a particular person?

Here's the spot-on bottom line on intuition:

If it feels good, do it, pursue it, follow it. It's meant for you. If it doesn't, don't. It's that simple. You have these feelings for a reason. And there's only one way to turn down the volume on them...which is to chronically ignore them until you don't feel anything anymore.

Warmer, warmer, burning up.

Using your intuition is like the game Hot and Cold. Did you ever play that when you were a kid? One player hides an object and then a second player has to find it. When the hunter gets closer to the object the other kids yell warmer, hot, about to get burned and so forth, and when the hunter is farther away from the object, the kids yell cooler, cold, and freezing! Intuition is like that. It signals to you with feelings rather than words. When you get closer to what you are meant to be doing, in any given moment, it feels warm and fuzzy. It feels exciting. When you get further away, it feels cooler, less comfortable, wrong, or ominous. As you move through your day, week, and life, God, the Universe, the Goddess, and your guides all yell "warmer" or "colder"- messages that show up as feelings in your gut. Excitement is a guide. Boredom, challenge, and discomfort are guides. No apparatus needed. You are enough.

There is a difference between giving in to fear, phobias and complacency and when the vibes are yelling colder. You might be afraid to trust the intuition you are getting because the outcome of a decision or situation is especially important to you and what your intuition is telling you to do requires courage. Your practical mind rolls though the scenarios, often settling on the worst case, and your logical mind runs endlessly through lists of pros and cons of all possible actions. You want a sure thing. You need a crystal ball. And the bottom line is that you don't trust yourself, including your gut. You have forgotten that you have survived 100% of the challenges you've faced.

Until you compared the results of trusting your gut and not trusting it, you won't have the evidence that shows you that your intuition is actually very, very good. And with its help you make great decisions.

You may be addicted to being comfortable even when comfortable isn't healthy for you. Your vibes may be trying to get you to take better care of yourself such as leaving the boyfriend who's just not that into you or the job where you're not appreciated, or to set boundaries with that toxic family member. But you're like, nah, I'm gonna stay right here. But when you decide it's time to make a move, trust your gut. Take your brain with you but let your vibes drive the car.

Not using your intuition is like trying to find your way out of a forest without using the compass that's tucked in your pocket. If I ask the U a question…

Before you go to sleep each night, think about a question you want answered or decision you must make. Ask for the answer. If you don't wake with the guidance you need the first night, keep trying. Keep a journal by your bed so you can write down dreams and messages. Write down any dream that seems peculiar, odd, uncannily realistic, symbolic or like the dream is trying to tell you something even if it seems unrelated to the knowledge you seek.

Here's an example. My husband, the kids, and I went to Europe in 2007. I had a strong feeling as soon as we returned home that I needed to get a full-time job. I wasn't worried when I was planning the trip or during the trip, but I woke up early the morning after our return, partly thanks to jet lag and partly thanks to intuition, and fixed up my resume. I emailed some of my contacts and let them know I needed a job. I had two interviews within a week, and two job offers from the interviews. One job was more of the work that I wanted to be doing in child development and assessment, but significantly less money and a lower level position than the second offer. The second was much more money, more responsibility, upper management, but a business position. I couldn't decide what to do, and my husband was supportive of whichever I chose. I wanted the work I felt more passionately about but thought it would be irresponsible to turn down the higher pay. I struggled with it for a couple days. I remembered about asking questions before sleep and the next night, I asked the question, "which job should I accept?" I woke up in the middle of the night with the strong feeling that I should take the business position and the higher pay. Thankfully, I listened to my intuition to get a job because the business partnership my husband was in imploded while we were in

Europe and he was forced to go back out on his own. Thankfully, I trusted my feeling about which job to take because the economic downturn in 2008 caused construction, and therefore, work for architects, to grind to a halt. We needed every bit of the money I was making to live on. The position turned out to be the right one for many other reasons as well.

I had felt a strong sense of intuition on other occasions such as the decision to stay home with my kids at the end of corporate job number one, and the decision for my husband to quit his day job and start his own business six months later. Yep, that meant neither of us had steady pay and no guarantees if we'd have enough money coming in to pay bills, but my gut said we'd be okay, so I trusted her. Same for taking the trip to Europe in 2007. We spent a small fortune for two weeks of amazing memories with our kids. If I had been psychic and known that our lives would become financially challenging for several years following that trip, I might have chosen not to take the trip. I might've let my practical mind, which would have told me to save that cash, win out. Our kids have become travelers and have had a priceless understanding of other cultures and the world since they were nine and twelve. I trusted my intuition to take the trip.

There have been many times when I didn't know exactly how things would work out but took a leap and trusted my vibes. It's difficult to follow your intuition when it's not in agreement with your logical, practical brain. My intuition and conscious mind have practically gotten into fist fights. They're both stubborn and each always think she's right.

So, what's the 5'1" Sicilian grandmother got to do with it?

She had a slew, and I mean a proverbial boatload, of superstitions, weird remedies from the old timers, and this notion that you got signs about things. She never called it intuition or any such thing, but she believed you got signs and you'd better pay attention to them. If you didn't, the signs would get more persuasive. She likened it to a cast iron frying pan to the head. (Before there was Teflon coated pans, there was cast iron.) If you heeded the signs at first, you could avoid bigger problems later. She had quite a few actual cast iron frying pans, from the little egg pans on up to the big ones you could cook a half pound of bacon in all at once. They were super heavy. And intuition doesn't use the little egg pans. It goes straight for the bacon. But if you pay attention sooner, you could avoid the blow. Kind of like, if you go to the dentist at the first sign of trouble, you might prevent the agony of realizing, in the middle of the night, that you need a root canal.

Also, don't walk under a ladder or step on cracks in the sidewalk. If you drop a knife, someone's coming to dinner, and if your palm itches, money is coming in. That's my favorite one! I still say that superstition to myself whenever my palm itches. I can't lie; it makes me excited. Somehow, I give no such attention to ladders, cracks, or black cats crossing my path. Optimist? Yes, I am. I take the superstitions that make me feel happy and leave the rest. I've said them to my kids enough so they know superstitions exist, out of respect to my nana and the dead relatives that came before her, and also because they play on in my head just like an old-time player piano. I've also taught my kids about intuition and cast iron, just as I'm teaching you.

Cast iron and more cast iron.

I've had the cast iron experience just a couple of times, and in looking back, I knew there were signs earlier that I chose to ignore. I paid attention later but wished I'd heeded sooner. The problem grew because I ignored it. Cast iron. Bacon pan.

First, before I share my bacon pan experiences, because it's only fair that I share them, I want to clarify that there's a difference between times when we have intuition that's (1) telling us not to do something and we do it anyway or (2) telling us to do something and we do not, in fact, do that thing- those situations are when we are asking for cast iron. We felt a nod in a particular direction and went the other way. There are also times when we don't bother to even check in with our intuition. We plow forward as if intuition isn't a thing. Some of us live substantial parts of their lives that way, right? We all know someone who thinks vibes are hogwash or woo-woo stuff. Or the cerebral folks who think science tells us to strictly use our gray matter. There are times where I've powered forward, forced to make a choice and I just jumped in with both feet. That would be how I was studying classical ballet one minute, then, seemingly forced to make a change in short notice, moved my ass over into the business college, with a goal of making money even if I had to sacrifice feeling passion to do it. I didn't even try to check with my gut on that one.

When my gut was loudly proclaiming "No! Don't."

I bought a used Mercedes. An older model. She was beautiful. I just wanted to hug her every time I saw her. In a way, it was a dream come true. It was in my vision scrapbook, and I had wanted a Mercedes ever since I was a kid watching Stephanie Powers character driving one on the series Hart to Hart, circa 1980. Jennifer Hart was stylish, smart, powerful, and married to an amazing guy. And she had the clothes and the car. Swoon.

The Mercedes, purchased from an acquaintance who proclaimed that "this engine is in the Smithsonian" however, the one in my car needed $10,000 in repairs in the first few months I had it. She was beautiful but my gut had said don't buy her. Do not fall for her beauty. And it was right. Cast iron. The big pan.

Second and third examples are also cars. My internal GPS was trying to steer me away. But I needed a car. Neither the BMW sedan nor the Toyota Camry wagon lasted more than a year. I got the signs. And looked the other way.

The remaining examples of when I did not trust my spidey sense fall into one category: worrying. I always feel in my gut that everything is as it should be and that everything is ok and will continue to be okay. That I feel inner wisdom telling me it's all good and yet, I still battle anxiety.

That I ever worry or have doubts is ludicrous. Life would be easier, for sure calmer, if I just trusted my gut. Like, always. Not just most of the time.

The most life changing magic has happened when I followed those vibes.

I pretty much always have. Here's a few examples. Within two weeks of meeting my now husband, I had a moment that felt like I was looking at a movie of my whole life. I looked at him and felt like I could see decades with him, if not centuries. Not something that normally happens to an eighteen-year old rebel girl who'd, earlier that day, sworn off men. I knew I wasn't supposed to let him go. I wasn't even looking for a guy when I met him, yet there he was, and my gut made sure I understood…hold onto him, troubled girl. All of the most monumental and the happiest times in my life have been the result of me trusting my inner nudges: moving to Florida, getting our cat George (when we weren't even allowed to have a pet!), getting a dog and eight years later a second dog- and in knowing which dogs were our family, deciding to get a boob job after being uncertain about it for years (I waited until my intuition gave me the green light in a dream!), going to Europe with my husband and taking the kids too, going to Paris, leaving my corporate jobs, studying psychology, my husband starting his own business, in choosing and nurturing friendships (I have three amazing besties), and in becoming a writer and coach. There are many more examples, but these are the biggies that were more than just a little right. No cast iron.

She's the girl everything works out for.

As an adult, I realized everything works out. Once you lived a few decades, you know that it does. If you're still living, everything has worked out. It may not have worked out the way you wanted or expected it to, but it has worked out or you'd be dead. You've undoubtedly found that there is always a silver lining if you bother to look for it. That's not just some idle rhetoric our mothers and grandmothers said. I decided to see if I could make even more things work out for me if that became my motto, "I'm the girl everything works out for." It's worked so far. Try it for yourself.

Everything I tell you is so that you can try what resonates with you and leave the rest. Of course, to do that, you must listen to your intuition. Feel the vibes. Feel what resonates with you. Feel the rain on your skin as Natasha Bedingfield says in the song Unwritten.

Ways to access your intuition.

Sway!

In *The Success Principles*, Jack Canfield shares how to do the Sway Test, which is based on the Law of Attraction, using your body as a way of getting an intuitive response. He states that in the same way a flower will grow toward the sun, your body possesses innate knowledge about what's best for you (Principle 47). "When you ask your body questions about what's right for you, it will lean backward or forward in response to your queries." In Principle 6, he explains that you stand with your feet together and hands at your sides. Ask your body what is a YES answer and wait until your body automatically moves forward or backward. Then clarify which is a NO answer, just to be certain it leans in the opposite direction. He further recommends that you test it out for accuracy by asking questions that you already know the yes or no answer to. When I tested my own body's calibration using the Sway test, I asked, "Is my name Lisa?" and "Do I have three children?" I immediately felt my body lean forward to the first and backward for no to the second. Both true. My name is Lisa, but I have two children, not three. I was shocked at how quickly my body leaned in a direction in response to a question when it was content to stand still or sway in a tiny circle in the absence of a question. I tested it several more times to make sure I was not doing the leaning consciously, like when you played with a Ouija board as a kid and wondered if it was the other person moving the planchette around. Seems to be legit.

If the Sway Test is how you access your intuition and it works for you, stellar. Use it. You may be wondering how else you can tune in to your intuition and be wondering if there are other ways it might speak to you. The answer is yes, there are many ways intuition can come through.

Maybe she'll pay attention to a billboard.

My intuition speaks to me in multiple ways. Most commonly, I see words on a billboard in my mind. I get answers immediately that way, usually before the question is fully asked, as if the typist already knew the question but needed me to begin to think it before answering. It makes sense that it can't answer questions I don't realize I'm asking! The answers are brief: one or two words if possible. I never get a whole paragraph. I also get feelings about things, like the game of hot and cold. Things will either feel good or bad, right for me or not right for me. I get vibes for other people and I can ask questions and get answers on other's behalf. One of my best friends gets intuitive guidance meant for me as well. It's hard to explain but it's a different feeling when it's for you and when it's for someone else. It feels less personal and sometimes less insistent when it's for someone else. Also, I can tell it's for her if it is a response to something I know she's been thinking about. If it doesn't make sense for me, it must be for her.

I also get answers in random places like signs I see in public and posts on social media. For example, I was driving to the bank one day and drove past a garden center. The message on the sign at the garden center, said, "Everything is better than you think." I had been worried about whether I was on the right path with my business or should I go back to a corporate job. I wasn't making much money, and my business wasn't growing as fast as I wanted it to. I was afraid I was ruining our financial future by taking this chance to make my dream come true. It had been a real test of my faith to keep going. And, still is occasionally! The message on the sign had absolutely nothing to do with plants or gardening! I had never seen this business post anything other than stuff about plants, what they had on sale, or the fact that they had just had puppies. Yes, they post on the sign at the garden center every time their dog has puppies.

I knew instantly that the sign was for me. I've been a manifestation maven for decades, so I didn't question it. But I know the normal response is probably, holy shit! Was that for me? And then you discount it talking about how many other people drove by that sign while it was up. Maybe it was for someone else. Or maybe it did have something to do with gardening that I couldn't figure out.

If it answers a question you've been wrestling with, it's for you. It's as simple as that. If it answers the question someone else who drove by it was also thinking about- could be a completely different question or struggle- but then yes, it was for her too.

That's how the Universe works. Signs for you will be put on your path. The U knows where you're going every single day, even before you do. And I don't know why the garden center owner thought he was putting that sign up there that day, but I do know it was for me. He got a gut feeling to do it. He acted on the hunch. I got my sign. Everything else is irrelevant.

Manifestation 101.

We can manifest everything we want from information and parking spaces on up to cars, houses, friends, partners, and a life we ridiculously fucking love! Everything. On that day, I manifested the answer to my question. Keep going. Everything is better than you think.

This has happened to me many times and my friends as well. One day, my friend drove by a church with a sign that said, "Why do you doubt me? -God" What was so remarkable is that my friend Liz was in a stressful crisis involving her young child and earlier that day, in complete turmoil, she had been yelling at God for a solution and some peace. She drove by that sign. If you think the sign is for you, and it relates to something that's been puzzling you, it's for you.

Back to other forms of receiving intuition and guidance.

Automatic writing also works for some. This kind of freeform writing involves being still, asking your question, and letting your hand write on the paper on its own. You don't need to be in a trance although this is not uncommon. Let your hand loosely grip a pen or pencil and let it write whatever it wants. Again, it will usually be simple answers, one or two words.

Those are some of the more common ways your intuition can talk to you, but how do you tune into it when yours seems to be whispering or permanently on silent?

---

1. **Meditate.** Busy-ness is the death of intuition. You must be still enough to hear it and feel it. While you may have to work at meditating to still your mind, it will happen with practice. You may want to choose guided meditations so that your mind has something to follow that is helping it to stay on track. Over time, meditating produces a homeostasis of inner calm even when not in active meditation. The inner calm is what turns up the volume on your vibes.
2. **Practice mindfulness.** Mindfulness is the practice of being still, paying attention to what's happening with you now and sensing how you're thinking and feeling. It's noticing tiny details of what's happening in the world around you now. A simple mindfulness exercise that I read about is to notice yourself eating food. Sit at the table with your food. No noise, no talking, no technology. Notice how you bite your food, how you chew it, how it tastes, and how you swallow it. Take your time and keep focused on the sight, smell, taste and feel of whatever you're eating. The goal here is to stay in the present moment and fine tune what you're aware of.
3. **Trust your vibes.** Not trusting yourself or your intuition is like turning the flame down on an oil lamp. You can't extinguish your intuition, but you can reduce it to a tiny flicker with distrust. Embrace that you have an internal guidance system. Play with it. Test it. Just

go with it. It's not a woo-woo thing (not that there's anything wrong with that) unless you make it one. Plenty of executives and CEOs make business decisions based on their hunches every day. In fact, most successful ones do, whether they talk about it or not.

4. **Write down what comes.** Keep an intuition journal. If you get a hunch, feeling, or message, write it down somewhere so that you can easily reference it later. The way to trust your vibes and increase your intuition is to be confronted with proof that you have good intuition. In the absence of proof, you will more easily remember when you feel your vibes were wrong than the dozens of times they were right. To be clear, your vibes are not wrong. You either asked the wrong question, got the context wrong or there's some other factor that influenced the outcome. Most of the time you will be spot on. Write it down.

5. **Express gratitude for the gift.** Being consciously grateful, on a regular basis, for the good in your life raises your vibration. A higher vibration increases your ability to feel, see, and hear your intuition. It increases your life satisfaction and happiness as well. In short, there are no unpleasant side effects for practicing gratitude. Be grateful for your intuition.

Whether you're inspired to heighten your intuition simply because it benefits you enormously to do so, or you're trying to avoid the cast iron, tune into it. Work on increasing your sensitivity and asking your gut questions more frequently. I'm not sure about the validity of any superstitions or that Mercurochrome and Witch Hazel can fix any ailment not cured with Calamine lotion or Bactine. But I am as certain about intuition as I am about many other things I learned from that 5'1" Sicilian grandmother, like how to make a great spaghetti sauce. My sauce speaks for itself and so does your intuition if you listen.

NOTES

Don't worry about black cats or stepping on cracks in the sidewalk, unless your intuition tells you to.

What I ridiculously love in this chapter:

The signs I've seen:

When my gut has been spot on:

Affirmation:

I trust my intuition and I trust myself. I am smart and kind and wise.

CHAPTER 13

Throw a Coming Out Party

"When in doubt, add more sparkle."

-Unknown

Who doesn't love a good coming out party? Feather boas not necessary. But who doesn't love a good feather boa also?

Even if you're not doing the "hey everybody, I'm gay!" sort of reveal, you still need to let everyone in on your giant, fantastic secret; the new you, new direction, and new life.

Announce the new you in a spectacular celebratory fashion. Here's why.

Reason Numero Uno.

The first reason is that in so doing, you seal the deal with yourself about your commitment. No going back. No reverting to what's comfy. No hasty retreat into the safety zone. Don't give yourself the option of being a pussy and making excuses about how the old you in your old haggard life (where on a good day you're just bored and on a bad day you contemplate jumping out the window until you remember your office is on the first floor and the window doesn't open) isn't so bad. Sigh. A party is a pronouncement, sealed with friends, family, and vodka. Or bourbon. And for sure champagne. The bigger the deal you make out of it, the less likely you are to go back in the closet wishing, wanting, and hoping for something you could definitely do, have, and be, if you weren't playing small and timid. Dress the part of who you are becoming and bask in the damn glow of it.

Secondly.

The second reason to throw one hell of a coming out party is to let God, the Universe, the Goddess, or whomever have faith in know you're READY. Intention is energy. "Like unto itself is drawn" according to the Law of Attraction. Remember? I think I've mentioned that once or twice already. Lol.

Let's Shazam! this shit.

You want to send out the energy of "bring it mothafucka!" Respectfully, of course. But the new you and new energy has to be slightly sassier than the old timid you who hid from her own shadow. Here's the deal: it's more than okay to realize that you do not want to stay where you are. You arrived in the spot you're in because you did the best you could with the resources you had at the time. You went to college, or not. You moved into the state, city, house you're in. You chose your career, vocation, or job. Or it chose you. Or your parents chose it, directly or indirectly. And you are the version of yourself because of the mental, spiritual, emotional, and physical resources you had in each moment where you made choices. This is based on who you were then. Those choices don't have to last a lifetime. They only have to last as long as they're making you happy. When a decision you made stops making you feel amazing, change it; don't be imprisoned with a life sentence.

We get so confused by what we think our past decisions mean in our lives. Stuck is always an illusion. The person who no longer wants to be stuck gets unstuck.

Move. You are not a tree.

Change one thing or everything. And throw a party to announce it. Let God know you're ready for the opportunities He or She has been waiting to send your way. Like, waiting for you to get off your ass and get ready to receive them. God can send all the opportunities to you, but until you take the first steps you won't notice them or worse, you'll notice them and let them sail right on by.

Get off your ass and out of your closet, Gorgeous.

Third reason and counting.

The third reason to throw a coming out party is that it will make you more accountable than you might otherwise be, especially if you don't have a coach. If you tell everyone about the new you, new work, new life, then you're much more likely to stick with it because you DO NOT want to have to tell all those people you wimped out, quit, or abandoned your dream. If you announce your dream coming true at a party, attendees will ask you how it's going from time to time. They'll ask you what's new. They'll want to know when your next article is coming out (me). They beg to know what you've accomplished lately because they're living vicariously through you and your big cajones. They'll be expecting you to volunteer updates as well. They will be inspired by you. They'll look up to you. Can you say peer pressure? And that's exactly what you need.

Last but certainly not least.

A coming out party allows people you care about to be supportive of the new you. You're not asking for their support because you can't move forward without it. That's permission not cheerleading. You're moving forward anyway, but you'll certainly take the bolstering if they offer it. Show me the love. <3

I had my coming out party at a family dinner where I promptly announced that I'm a writer. Not that I want to become a writer, that I'm contemplating being a writer, or that I hope to become a writer. I announced that I am a writer. I went in the closet and got out my big balls for that party.

I didn't have a single thing published at that time, but I had a lot written and I knew by the resonance in my soul (and confirmation from a psychic because why not) that writing is the correct outlet to fulfill my purpose of helping people. Now I have done lots of things, held several different kinds of jobs, had a collection of college degrees and certifications, which if you merely glanced at it looks like I can't make up my mind. My resume and college transcripts look like I can't stick to just one thing. Not admirable qualities. Jack of all trades, master of none is never a compliment. However, if you know what I do, it all fits together as if planned by an entity higher than myself, who knew what I needed to do in order to become who I am meant to be. No shit. And when I announced it at family dinner, no one batted an eye. They rallied around me in the most supportive way. It was very natural. Like, of course you're a writer. I had an article published a month later.

Become it before you become it.

The day that article was published in an online magazine was one of the best days of my entire life. Better than the first time I went to Disney World or Europe, better than graduating from college, not quite as magical as my wedding day or the days my babies were born, but really fucking spectacular. I felt like I was vibrating. I felt like I had hearts and sunshine all around me. That good. I still get super excited every time I have an article published, and I haven't even made it into *O* Magazine or *Glamour* yet. Or *Forbes*. I will probably pass right out when that happens. But when I come to, hearts and sunshine. The support of my family is everything, but I would have to do this anyway. Writing is in my soul. I don't even know where the words come from sometimes.

Oh, the pressure.

The support wasn't the propeller though, the peer pressure was. I proclaimed my new life to everyone and that's what sealed the deal so that I'd see it through. It still does. I can't quit because it's in my soul. I also can't quit because I don't want to disappoint those I inspire, including those who have endorsed my dream and those who read my articles, blogs, and hopefully this book. I've been writing this book for three years. That's a long time to believe in myself, hone my craft, deal with frustration on days where I'm too anxious or depressed for the words to come, make myself take needed breaks from writing, and most of all to pray that these are exactly the words you need to hear.

My girlfriends all say they hear me in their heads, and though we laugh about that, I know what they mean. Abigail lets me know when articles, posts, and chapters don't sound like me. Sometimes I'm off because depression is showing up in my work. Sometimes it's a slight disconnection from my real self who is willing to stand out, to say the difficult things in the very genuinely caring, witty way that that are true to me. My friends laugh a lot around me, so I believe them that the work needs to be more me.

Throwing the coming-out party launched me forward with the force of a cannon fired. I couldn't wait to produce a newsworthy accomplishment. Then another. I give regular updates, where natural and not obnoxious, because it holds me accountable. I produce articles regularly because then, in addition to seeing my words in print, I get to announce the accomplishment and validate to everyone that I'm working hard and very much still on my path. This is important. I'm a role model. Each of us is a role model to those around us. You never know who you're inspiring so make sure you are doing inspiring things. Live your very best life.

Imposter Syndrome is real.

In a Harvard Business Review article, imposter syndrome was defined as "a collection of feelings of inadequacy that persist despite evident success." And goes on to explain, "Imposters suffer from chronic self-doubt and a sense of intellectual fraudulence that override any feelings of success or external proof of their competence." Rather than a by-product of low self-esteem, imposter syndrome is more likely to afflict those who are perfectionists and feel like they will never be good enough, credentialed enough or experienced enough. You control your thoughts. You are not a fake. And you're not just lucky. You are becoming who you are meant to be. You're already her; your becoming fully her. Not a fraud.

As with all thought control, acknowledge the thoughts, look for evidence that what you are thinking is true or not true, and if they aren't true, quit thinking it. Contemplate whether this is your inner perfectionist talking.

The expert conundrum.

At what point are you an expert? What credentials do experts have? It seems that some people easily refer to themselves as experts while others refuse to self-define as such. I have to admit that I had trouble referring to myself as an expert. Coming from a research background, I had a mental model of experts as having PhD or MD after their names and decades of narrowly focused experience in a subject area. I don't know any PhDs however who use the term expert. There's always someone who knows more than you do. But, and it's a big but, when you are marketing your business, people want to know that you're an expert in whatever your teaching. It's part of how they trust you; the T part of the KLT, know/like/trust factor that you must have with your customers. Trust includes being consistent and competent.

I saw a hot debate on social media while writing this book about the use of the word expert. I decided, as I so often do, to defer to my gal pal Merriam, to see what she has to say about it. After all, we would consider Merriam an expert, wouldn't we?

Merriam defines expert as: (1) one with the special skill or knowledge representing mastery of a particular subject; (2) having, involving, or displaying special skill or knowledge derived from training or experience. This only led to more questions. What's mastery then? She defines mastery as "possession or display of great skill or technique." I find all this as completely subjective as the online debate I witnessed. There doesn't seem to be a concrete, "you'll know when you've arrived" definition. So, if you have mastery in an area and want to call yourself an expert go for it. If you prefer to let your haute competence speak for itself without a label, do that. Do what makes you happy.

Back to party planning.

How are you going to come out? Who will be invited? What will the theme be? What will you wear? Will it be black tie, a Hawaiian luau or hoedown?

Whatever it is, dress the part. Take pictures of the new you in the Louboutins, grass skirt and lei or cowboy boots and put those pictures on your vision board. Accept the support and accolades. Assume the persona. You aren't an imposter and you're not faking it. You're becoming it. You're making it real, setting the intention and directing your energy. The opportunities have no choice but to come to you. Look ready so you fully feel ready. Invite others to come to the party as the person they'd like to be in a year or two. Tell them they can change one thing or everything. Come as they want to be and not as they are. We are not trees. We can move as many times as it takes.

Life is good. Have your cake and eat it too. And do throw a party.

NOTES

Big tribe or small, find your friends and tell them all.

What I *ridiculously* love in this chapter:

Party Date:

Party Details:

What I will wear:

Affirmation:

I celebrate my new life and new me. I share my joy with others.

CHAPTER 14

Regret Is a Motherfucker

"Regret for the things we did can be tempered in time; it is regret for things we did not do that is inconsolable."
-Sydney J. Harris,
American journalist and author

What do you think you will regret if you never do it?
Having children?
Earning a college degree?
Travelling to your dream destination?
Learning to paint?
Writing your memoir?
Reconnecting with friends or family members?
Healing old wounds?
Finding the love of your life?
Starting your own business?

Maybe it's having more adventures. Feeling that fear and doing it anyway. Maybe it's living each day to its fullest, burdens lifted. Perhaps it's to be happier.

For me, I know very clearly that if I didn't write and become a life coach, helping others have a better outlook on life, love, happiness, I'd regret it. This is not only what I have trained to do but what feels so good that I know I've tapped into my purpose. If I were to give in to my insecurities about being good enough, being rejected by publishers, being heckled by trolls, or thinking that I don't know enough, I'm 100% certain I would regret it.

If at the end of my life I wonder "what if I had just done it" about anything, I will feel regret and sorrow. I get slightly teary-eyed now just thinking about it. My goal is to be a number one *New York Times* bestselling author. And I want to sit with Oprah and talk about my books. I need to achieve these things to have no regrets at the end of my life. I need to write for you, to help you have a happier life. If I don't do this, I will be wasting the gifts that I was given. I was given a love of words, intuition, compassion, and a will to help others feel better mentally, emotionally, and spiritually.

I must honor the experiences I've had: abandoned by my father, being abused and neglected by my mother, shown that not everyone is bad by my nana and pop, feeling the passion I had for dance, the absence of passion for business, the mind-blowing experience of having children, studying psychology, training as a coach with Anthony Robbins, discovering my calling as a writer, finding an amazing soul mate who supports me in making my dreams come true, and having friends who believe in me and refer to me as "our Oprah." I know that these experiences were no accident but all part of my path. No plot twist arrived late. In diving timing, there is only right on time.

The Universe operates in accordance with diving timing. This is a relief. I never have to feel like I was late figuring out any part of my life. I believe we choose our lives in all the glorious detail before we're born. Sarcastically, I question my prenatal choices and the level of difficulty I chose. Maybe all the cards that said "easy life with adoring parents" were taken when it was my turn to draw. That said, knowing me like I do, there was probably a card that said, "meaningful life that will be effortless eventually once you learn to surrender" and I picked that one. Just like in the gym, I don't choose easy. I always prefer badass.

Many times, I've wondered why I didn't discover psychology first instead of business. I could have gotten my Ph.D. and been a psychologist and had an amazing life. Not to mention I could've skipped all the student loans I'm still paying on to pursue what I didn't love. The psychologist path from dance major wasn't meant to be.

The timetable? Dance in 1985, business degree and grad studies done by January 1994. Married in August 1994. My daughter was born in June 1995 and my son followed in February of 1998. I earned my psychology degree in 2007 followed by multiple years of rejection to clinical psychology PhD programs. I began coach training in 2012, entering a master's program in psychology in 2013 and launched Small Steps 2 Big Change in 2014. I got my first article published in 2014 and launched my website/blog and coaching services in 2014 as well. I had the concept for Small Steps 2 Big Change, which came to me in a dream as many things have, well before 2012.

Corporate job number one, 1994-2000.

Corporate job number two, 2007-2014.

Before stepping into owning my life as a writer and coach, I looked at all I had done and thought it seemed haphazard, like I just couldn't make up my mind what I want to be when I grow up (except that I was in my thirties and then forties). I surmised that I have too many interests and not enough commitment. Then I got fired from corporate job number two. And again, as in 2000 when corporate job number one ended, I had a moment to myself to take a long look at things.

I realized my path isn't desultory at all. Or undecided. What if I'd been given the exact experiences I was meant to have, when I was meant to have them, with the exact right people, so that I could fulfill my destiny? What if it was all beautifully synchronous? It was.

Holy shit moment!

What I learned-

What and who you are meant to be is always whispering to you but is often amplified by events and people who show you what and who you are and what and who you are not. They're all important. If you hold the thought each morning, "I will happily learn more of who I am today," it will come.

Regret is a mother fucker. A mirror. A teacher.

Regret is a motivator. #gratitude

I could feel impending regret each time I took a corporate job. My soul was whispering not this.

My education and experience, the practical brain, said "yes, this." My purpose, and therefore my passion, not being ones to wrestle with "logic," took seats in the back. Never for long. It seems they will only wait seven years at a time because that's the point where both of my corporate jobs ended, not of my own doing. Not of my own conscious doing anyway. Consciousness, you know, where practicality dominates. I'm sure, subconsciously, I was calling in an escape.

I could feel the tug of a purpose, growing restless for a year or two before the ends, to the extent that I started Small Steps 2 Big Change months before I was released from my last corporate cage. I was in graduate school, at that time, for psychology. I spent the latter eight months of 2014 recovering from the stressful work environment, rebuilding my strength and spirit, and planning for the future.

On November 28, 2014, I wrote a journal entry turned blog post that began with the following question:

"What do you have to change before this time next year or you just might die?"

Perhaps "die" is a little dramatic, but it's pretty close to what I really mean. What is the one (or ten) thing you have to change so you don't hate your life and yourself for not going for your dream?"

It was a long, heartfelt post, documenting my looming regret that my purpose will go unfulfilled or fulfilled in a smaller way than intended. Smaller than my soul demands. That knowing my what, who, and why might not be enough to combat my fear, doubts, and anxiety that were making me play small while what I want is very big. I would tell myself things like, "I don't know how to…" (disempowering belief) and thinking, "why would anyone want to help me figure it out unless I'm paying them" (rejection complex). Shit sandwiches. There's been very little I haven't been able to figure out and people are generally willing to help if I ask them.

Fast forward to November 2015. I have articles published in Huffington Post. The beginnings of establishing myself as a writer on a bigger platform where I could be criticized or embraced as a writer. I knew I was continuing to play small and hoping there would be more time and opportunity. I still felt pissed off at myself for this year-end inventory of where I was versus where I wanted to be.

Thankfully, the fear of regret is big enough to push me past all my other fears. Past fear of failure. Zoomed right on by fear of success. Dodged "I'm not good enough." I knew my tribe was hanging out online. I really had no idea how to be a virtual entrepreneur. While I'm good at many things, technology isn't one of them.

On December 15, 2015 (yes, right before Christmas), I invested in an online business coach. I had been hanging out in her Facebook group for some time. I knew she could show me many of the things I didn't know. I saw it as my chance to make more progress before December 31st. Because I signed up when I did, I got access to another coach and learned even more of what I needed to know about being visible and selling online. As with all the teachers who have, throughout my life, appeared at just the right time, to shine light on my path, I am forever grateful to these two coaches. We hit the ground running on December 16th, luckily, because regret was chasing me.

Thankfully, regret is a motherfucker. If you haven't been sufficiently motivated by anything else, I hope regret is your mother fucker too. I pray that it moves you toward your purpose, your passion, peace, and a life you ridiculously love.

I hope you feel the possibility of regret of not doing "it" as boldly and terrifyingly as I do.

I do not fear regretting what I do- even if it doesn't work out. I do not fear failure. I fear that I might have to regret not going all in.

Do not ever worry that you are too old, too undecided, or anything else. Everything is as it's meant to be, every minute of your life. When you stop cursing perceived delays, you will see, often in hindsight, the timing of everything is perfect for you. If you're reading this book, I know that you're looking for something you don't have but feel exists. I know you're trying to put your puzzle pieces together, to step into your purpose and feel the sheer joy that comes with it. You can't buy the blueprint of your life online, rush it, or get it in any store. Not even amazon.com. But you can figure it out.

Researchers state that regret is experienced in relation to opportunities. Where opportunities are denied or where problematic circumstances are inevitable, you can rationalize away regret. Where opportunity remains viable, the possibility of regret is high.

Researchers also acknowledge that regret "pushes people toward revised decision making and corrective action that often bring about an improvement in life circumstances." Regret on inaction persists longer than regret of action taken. So, you are more likely to regret not doing something than doing it but not getting the outcome you desired.

This is why you should be like Nike and JUST DO IT!

Literally, just do it.

So, regret makes you feel bad about yourself but can also be the motivational factor to get you to remedy the situation before it causes the regret. Whether you act or not depends on if you believe there is an opportunity to act and whether those actions will be effective.

Even if you have suffocated your feelings over the years so that you could continue to play small, be dedicated to others, be practical, tolerant, and be someone who is only some diminished version of your whole self, now is the time to unleash. I get it.

So many of us put our true heart's desire on hold as we build careers, have children, and hopefully find who we are along the way. But you also know the altercation to which I refer, the place where the soul begins to speak louder than practicality. It whispers at first. Eventually it gets louder and more boisterous. More insistent. It may even bring cast iron. You're meant to listen to it. There are no accidents. There are no coincidences. You have a soul, a destiny, and a purpose. And regret looks, sounds, smells, and unmistakably feels like a mother fucker.

Thank God for that.

NOTES

You have this day right here. Make it a great one.

What I *ridiculously* love in this chapter:

What I know I will regret if I never do it:

How will it feel if I do it? What would it be life if I go "all in?"

Affirmation:

I will live my life fully. I do this for me. I am worthy of all that I want. I am enough.

Epilogue. And shameless plug for the next book where we go deeper.

So, we've had our first journey together. My hope is that it's just the beginning; that you feel a renewed connection with yourself. I hope that you feel relieved, empowered, activated, connected and hopeful-REACH. I hope that you now know that you have the power to reach all you desire. Get what you want and don't feel guilty for it. When you are your whole self you are your best self and everyone around you benefits in so many ways.

Relieved.

I pray that you feel relieved that the future is yours to create. The past, whatever it brought, does not accurately predict your future. The future is all you; let your dreams fully loose. You know that regret is not inevitable but can be a powerful ally propelling you forward. Do not ignore her; befriend her. Be emboldened by her. May you also feel relieved that the wonder of your inner child is still within you. Embrace it. No matter how big or small your dream, if you're dreaming it then it's meant for you. And you're not alone. We all have a purpose, our soul's mission, and it speaks to us through that which we feel passionately about. You are given the desires meant for you. Passion for what is yours to do, have and become. All of it. You may need to welcome opportunities, hone your skills and change some of your current beliefs about yourself and the world, but the seeds of all you need are in every cell of you the same as your DNA. Relief.

You will most certainly feel the relief that comes with mastery over your negative self talk and your ability to embrace self-love with zero tolerance for anything less. Do not talk shit about yourself. You are, each day, doing the best you can with the mental, emotional, spiritual and physical resources you have. When you struggle, feel stressed or depressed, it is only a calling to do what you now know how to do, to bolster those resources. Do not get overwhelmed by it for more than a minute. Do not berate yourself for even a single second. Boost yourself. Rekindle your spirit. This is the perfect time to connect; not to lament, but to share and allow others to remind you who you are. Go for a walk in nature. Hit the gym. Check your boundaries. Are they where they need to be or do they need a self-protective tightening? Happiness is not the absence of other emotions, but the kind-hearted acceptance of them while knowing your home base.

Empowered.

You are your own fairy godmother. And thank God for that! You have you for the rest of your days. If you want it, get it. Get what you want. Get clear about what you want. Crystal clear. Starry night clear. What gives your life meaning? What will you regret if you don't do it, be it and have it? What will you regret if you do not go all in on it? You have a party to plan. New you, new life. Change one thing or everything. All that you are powering through, putting up with and tolerating suggests change. You don't want a shoulder shrug life; you want jazz hands. Disco night. Sequins. Glitter. And you have all that you need within you. If you weren't you, you'd want to be you. See it, feel it, smell it and, most of all, taste the deliciousness of all you will create. The days of classifying, quantifying, qualifying and criticizing yourself, what you want to do and have are so over. Do not judge yourself. And for all that is holy, do not feel guilty about what you want. Guilt sucks. Like, it always sucks. Guilt doesn't ever not suck. Let your dreams unfold. Embrace your wonderful, witty, whacky, soulful, fun, funny, mundane, flamboyant, amazing self. You are amazing, in the true sense of the word. You deserve all that you dream of. If you dream it, it's for you. Really, Gorgeous, get what you want.

Activated.

You now know that your possibilities are endless. It's not enough to know it. You must take a step. Then pause to feel the energy and exhilaration of that step. Feel the sheer power of it. Take in the comfort of it. Enjoy the joy. Journal those feelings. Then take another step. You do not need grand gestures or big leaps, though they are good too. There is much power in the small steps. I feel so strongly about the magnitude of small steps that I named my company Small Steps 2 Big Change. I was a dancer and I love the grace and strength required for a grand jete but there is just as much quiet strength in small steps.

Each morning ask yourself, "what must I accomplish today to feel great tonight?" The goal is to get to the evening hours and not feel disappointed, or worse, the need to anesthetize with a bottle of wine and a credit card. Becoming who you are meant to be has no nasty side effects. Doing what you are meant to do equals enduring happiness. Document each accomplishment. Celebrate your progress. Do not give in to your excuses. If you want it, get it. Do it. Have it. Become it. Do at least one small step every day.

You win if you begin and then just don't quit.

Connected.

No one, and I mean no one, gets where she wants to go alone. Connect with other like-minded people. Find your soul sisters and brothers. Most of all, keep company with people who are also doing, having and becoming more. Those are the ones who will truly understand your journey. Connect with those on similar spiritual paths. These don't all have to be the same five or ten people. Your spiritual tribe may not be your philanthropical group, who may not be your fellow entrepreneurs or business besties. Your tribe will likely consist of many unrelated smaller tribes in which you are the common thread. The important bit about your tribe is that they are of your choosing, unlike family. Jim Rohn famously said that, "you are the average of the five people you spend the most time with." When you look at those five people, how many of them are where you want to be? I'm not telling you to ditch all your current friends or to tell your family to fuck off. I am telling you to be deliberate and conscious about who you are giving your time, energy and money to. I'm telling you to build your tribe. I'm offering that it is better to hang out with an inspiring book than an uninspiring coworker. It's better to say no thank you to what you don't want than to hope you can find precious additional seconds for what you do want. Connection with your tribe can occur any way you can get it. Books, audiobooks, movies, interviews, podcasts, newsletters, Facebook groups, emails, text messages, live chats, classes, workshops, volunteer work and in so many other ways. Be deliberate. Decide. Limit your time, energy and money to what makes you more you. Think of it like math if math resonates with you. You want all sums. No subtraction. If it adds to you, do it. If it takes away from you, don't do it or do as little of it as possible.

This may sound like I'm saying don't help others; though if you've read this book, you know, that helping others in some way is the center of all our purposes. It's the only mission that exists. The means by which we help is the variable for which we are uniquely suited. But in case you're one of those that reads the ends of books before the beginnings and middles, you are now clear that we must give our time, energy and money to help people, animals and everything else on the planet in the ways that we feel drawn. And those who are on similar paths are our people. And we must unapologetically say no to what we might be good at, able to easily do, the only one willing to do something, if it is not something to which we feel a resonance. When we are not rescuing, enabling, and championing endless tasks others could do (or not), we have more time and energy for what is meant for us. Live purposefully. Find your tribe. And really, love them hard. Cliché. But worthwhile.

Hopeful.

I often contemplate what I want my readers to feel. The hallmark of a good speech is that it sticks to this articulation plan: what do you want your audience to know, how do you want them to feel, and what do you want them to go do. I believe that everything I write must have this structure as well. Do not take up space on a page trivially and, most importantly, do not waste your audience's time. But, why do I write? It would be easy to say that I write because I love words but then I might write fiction, fantasy or some other useful diversion from real life. Something with a future opportunity for me to sell the movie rights. Something that pairs well with wine, couches and credit cards. And, while that sounds lovely, I write no fiction. Then there is my background and education in both business and psychology, which screams self-help. While this is a natural fit of skills for sure, and pairs well with a love of words, there is one reason I write for you. Hope. The single most powerful gift you can offer someone is hope. I want you to know you're not alone in the world or in your experience of it, and I want to restore your hope that the future can be better than the past and can be as amazing as you can dream it to be. Is this all there is? No, dear one. There is so much more. I'm only telling you what you already know is true. You've felt the tug of greater things that you must do. Suspend your disbelief. And know what you love and like. Know what you do not love and do not like. Then decide you will change whatever needs changed. What and who must go. Set down the tremendous weight you've been carrying. Lay down decades old responsibility to be perfect, to care for EVERYONE, to never ever make a mistake. Shed what has made you think you are less than divinely ordained. You want to know what freedom feels like? Smile and make eye contact everywhere you go. Say hello and how are you and listen for an answer. Hold the door. Don't rush to walk or drive behind a car backing out of a parking space. Breathe. Delight in this moment right here and in whomever shares it with you.

We have this unnecessary urgency about everything as if we're always about to be late. We're too busy to take time for people. We take everything as a personal assault. We ascribe so much to ourselves that is, not only not meant for us, but literally has not a single damn thing to do with us. The person that cuts you off in traffic is not trying to cause harm to you or your car. Maybe he's reckless or maybe he found out he lost his job today. Maybe she's just not paying attention or maybe she's thinking about her son who is struggling in school. Perhaps she's late for work and will get fired if she's late again. Maybe he has cancer, or his child does. Most of what other people do is not remotely about you. And you don't know their stories. You have a choice in how you react or respond. You can wish them well and pray they get to their destination safely while being thankful you have lightning quick reaction time and great brakes. Or you can get angry, call them names they'll never hear and let the elevated physiology and cortisol have its negative impact on your body. React in the moment to a perceived assault or respond by staying in your Zen zone. The happiest version of you stays in her Zen zone with the insight you now have about why we think, act and feel the way we do. You know we have this mix of personality traits (openness to experience, extroversion, neuroticism, agreeableness and conscientiousness), life experiences that have been filtered through the lens of our individual inheritances of those traits, and our mental ideal of how the world behaves which was formed based on those personality characteristics and experiences. And our earliest experiences determined how our brains were wired- stability and nurture or flight and fight. This makes us who we are with mental, emotional, physical and spiritual resources that are bountiful or scare. Some days on top of the wave and some days under it hoping that we can punch our way or at least float to the surface again. Experiences we label as good and bad happen to everyone. In actuality, they are neither good nor bad, they're just life. We feel hope when we know how to restore these resources to their optimal levels. Better yet if we have reserves, we can share with others who need a lift. Yes, hope to share. To do this we must start with small steps. Kindness, patience, responses not reactions. Zen. Be the role model. Emotions and behavior are contagious. Inspire others with your manner and actions. This is what hope looks like on a daily basis. A hope that we desperately need right now. If we cannot look to our leaders, we can still look to ourselves. There was a time when honor predominated our culture. And trust. You were taken at your word. Trust was given freely until someone demonstrated themselves not to be trustworthy and this was not the norm. People helped each other. Kindness was as commonplace as anger and impatience are today. As we have cared less about others, we have become more anxious and depressed than at any other time in our history. Coincidence? No, it is not. Hope cannot be gained solitarily. Just the opposite. Hope is derived from the principle that we are better together, and we cannot be together if we cannot be kind and patient with one another. If we are too busy for common courtesy. Too busy to help our neighbors, friends and communities.

If we cannot look to our leaders, fear not, because we can look to ourselves. We are the hope we are missing. We are most definitely better together. The other reason I write for you is connection. I am calling in my tribe. Are you with me? As we change ourselves to fulfil our greater purpose, we change the world.

I am your big change coach. And I'm right here with you and for you.

You are worthy.

You are enough.

"These gifts I give unto you, greater work shall you do." The words that have played over and over in my head for decades. It is not only my purpose calling urgently, it's yours too.

And so the journey continues.

This book is called Get What You Want because Alexa says so. Because my then-twelve-year old handed me a life lesson in a McDonald's drive thru. I would prefer to say that it happened somewhere lovelier like Elizabeth Arden's Red Door Salon, on the balcony of our hotel room in Barcelona or in our majestic suite on the Mediterranean cruise where so many shenanigans occurred. Comedy club. No. We don't get to choose where our life-changing lightbulb moments happen. So, McDonald's drive thru it was. More importantly, we do get to choose whether we pay attention to them or let them fly right past. "Get what you want mom." So clear to a 12-year-old, as things often are. It was the beginning of the journey from tired pushover to purposeful powerhouse. I knew if I needed to learn how to find my way back, others must need it too.

Along the way, I realized that getting what you want (not even remotely about taking from others because abundance is real) is a formula with three equally important parts: getting clear about what you want, getting real about where you are now versus where you want to be and what has to change, and getting going because wishing and wanting something until the cows come home won't bring it to you. I also realized, because I started asking people "well, what do you want" that most of the time they don't know. Or they have some very unspecific, global notion of what they want. Or they can only tell me what they don't want…debt, more fucking stuff to deal with, etc. Well if you don't know what you want, how do you expect to get it? And how will you know if you do? Maybe you already have what you want and you just don't know it.

In this book, Get What You Want: How to Get Clear, Get Real and Get Going, I introduced you to the concepts of clarity, reality and action but spent most of my word count teaching you how to let go of some of the stuff that's been holding you back, kind of like cleaning out closets and making room for newer and better. I used the rest of this book's page count to help you to get clear. Like I always say, we must begin at the beginning. Clarity about what makes you happy is the first step.

That said, there is another layer. There are thirteen amazing chapters in this book but there were thirty-six original chapters in total. Yes, I wrote the War and Peace of self-help. Some 500 pages. Which no one, including me, wants to read. That said, there is more. Which brings me to the shameless plug for the next book in the Get What You Want series. In the next volume, Unleash Your Inner Badass, we will focus more on getting real with chapters such as: Liking Change So Much You Seek It Out in Dark Alleys and Seedy Neighborhoods and the Cognitive Dissonance Problem (Yes You Have One). We will also focus on getting going with chapters like Herd Your Squirrels (How to Turn Your Squirrels Into A Wolf Pack And Get What You Want) and Off With Your Training Pants, You're A Big Kid Now (Even If You Still Feel Like You Might Shit Yourself On Occasion). This book will continue your training. There will be shenanigans. And cocktail references. And light swearing. Just the same as if you were hanging out with me. Only then there'd be shenanigans, probably not-so-light swearing, actual cocktails and lots of laughs while talking about life. Know your girlfriends, keep them close, love them hard. You want to survive being a mom? Girlfriends. You want to survive living with men (who are from Mars)? Girlfriends. Commiserate about your soul-sucking job? Girlfriends. Remember who you are when you don't recognize the tired, older, life-sucked out of you version of yourself in the mirror? Girlfriends. Talk to someone who always thinks you're fucking awesome, when no one else seems to think so? Girlfriends.

And, speaking of girlfriends, when you seem them next…bring them this book. And the next book. Change your lives together. Let them be the five people who bring up that fucking average of who you all are. Take that, Jim Rohn.

You've got this. Really. You do. You are FUCKING AWESOME!
And I'm right here with you cheering you on.

Hugs and Love.

Want more of me right now?

Follow me on social media. (Please…)

Instagram: @bigchangecoach
Twitter: @bigchangecoach
Facebook: @smallsteps2bigchange

And be sure to head on over to **www.smallsteps2bigchange.com** to download my Free guides on everything happiness and success, to get my newsletters so you know what's happening next, for blog posts and how you can work with me… if you want me all to yourself.

#womenmeantformore
#getwhatyouwant

And check out my course on confidence:

UNLEASH YOUR INNER BADASS

30 DAYS TO A CONFIDENT YOU

Visit www.smallsteps2bigchange.com for details.

My Bucket List

1. Have my book hit #1 on the NY Times Best-seller list.
2. Have a book I wrote translated into over 40 languages and be an international best seller.
3. Learn to be a great speaker (in progress)
4. Become fluent in French
5. Learn conversational Spanish
6. Learn conversational Italian
7. Learn to take great photos
8. Visit Puerto Rico
9. Vacation in France at least once a year until I no longer want to
10. Learn to play the piano
11. ~~Visit the Met Costume Institute~~
12. Go on a dinosaur dig
13. ~~See humpback whales~~
14. See blue whales
15. See Whale Sharks
16. Get Rosemary's Bears going and be a successful nonprofit
17. Do a Ted Talk that gets at least 4 million views
18. Be an O Magazine Insider and Brand Ambassador
19. Be named one of Oprah's Thought Leaders
20. Meet Oprah
21. Meet Tony Robbins
22. Do projects that help people or animals with 20 & 21
23. Help with animal conservation and education
24. Help kids in the foster care system in a bigger way

25. Play the flute again
26. Write a memoir.
27. Write a series of books for and get them published
28. Be able to make plants flourish in my care
29. Create books and a program that help teens and 20 somethings find their way, especially ones without parents or estranged from their parents/caregivers.
30. Create a legacy
31. Have a spiritual practice that's so well ingrained that I no longer need anxiety to remind me of things I forget but need not to. (In progress)
32. Learn to swim without holding my nose
33. Be able to do a cartwheel again (and maybe a handstand)
34. Show others that anything is possible at any age
35. Run a marathon
36. Develop a signature cocktail- the Lisatini? Bourbonista?
37. Stay at the Grand Floridian at Disney World
38. Visit California Disneyland
39. See all the countries in western Europe that I haven't been to yet.
40. Learn to speak a little Russian
41. Visit the cemeteries where my favorite old movie stars are buried. Forest Lawn and Hollywood Forever, etc.
42. Shop on Rodeo Drive
43. Visit a movie studio in Cali (and see the costume department and archives)
44. Own a Balenciaga or Oscar de la Renta (or both) ball gown
45. Own a Chanel suit
46. Own a Gianni Versace original
47. Own a Louis Vuitton bag
48. Visit Tiffany & Co in Manhattan

49. Visit where Mom Moms apartment was on West 22nd Street in Manhattan (better get the address from Aunt Rosalie)
50. Have an occasion to wear a ball gown
51. ~~Own a pair of Manolo Blahnik shoes~~
52. See a Broadway show on Broadway
53. See the New York City Ballet at Lincoln Center
54. See the American Ballet Theater
55. Be known as a great humanitarian
56. Take ballet, tap, hip hop and pointe classes
57. Interview and write about ballet dancers- some aspect of their lives
58. Do some photojournalism- maybe about fashion or something like Humans of NY- telling people's stories
59. See Olympic gymnastics events
60. Get an honorary PhD from a good university
61. Win an award for my writing
62. Be known as a style icon
63. Get my master's degree in social work or mental health counseling
64. Be a respected expert in the fields of happiness and success
65. Learn to day trade and make money for myself
66. Take singing lessons so I maybe could carry a tune in a bucket list. Or learn for sure that it's impossible for me.
67. Have a reading with Theresa Caputo, Tyler Henry or John Edward
68. Be a UN Ambassador
69. Attend midnight mass in one of the beautiful cathedrals in Europe.
70. Do a stand-up comedy routine or write for a comedy show

RESOURCES

Aka. Stuff I Ridiculously Love So You Might Too.

BOOKS:

Abraham, et al. *The Law of Attraction: the Basics of the Teachings of Abraham.* Hay House, 2007.

Bernstein, Gabrielle. *The Universe Has Your Back: Transform Fear to Faith.* Hay House, Inc., 2016.

Canfield, Jack, and Janet Switzer. *The Success Principles: How to Get from Where You Are to Where You Want to Be.* William Morrow, an Imprint of HarperCollinsPublishers, 2015.

Duckworth, Angela. *Grit: the Power of Passion and Perseverance.* Scribner, 2018.

Duffield-Thomas, Denise. *Lucky Bitch: a Guide for Exceptional Women to Create Outrageous Success.* CreateSpace, 2012.

Dweck, Carol. *Mindset the New Psychology of Success.* Ballantine Books, 2016.

Ford, Debbie. *The Dark Side of the Light Chasers: Reclaiming Your Power, Creativity, Brilliance, and Dreams.* Riverhead Books, 1999.

Frankl, Viktor E., et al. *Mans Search for Meaning.* Beacon Press, 2019.

Hoff, Benjamin. *The Tao of Pooh.* Penguin Books, 1986.

Knight, Sarah. *The Life-Changing Magic of Not Giving a f*Ck: How to Stop Spending Time You Don't Have with People You Don't like Doing Things You Don't Want to Do.* Little, Brown and Company, 2015.

Lyubomirsky, Sonja. *The How of Happiness: a New Approach to Getting the Life You Want.* Penguin Books, 2008.

Seligman, Martin E. P. *What You Can Change and What You Can't the Complete Guide to Successful Self-Improvement.* Vintage Books, 2007.

Seligman, Martin E. P. *Flourish: A Visionary New Understanding of Happiness and Well-Being.* Atria Paperback, 2013.

Seligman, Martin E. P. *Authentic Happiness: Using the New Positive Psychology to Realize Your Potential for Lasting Fulfillment.* Atria Paperback, 2013.

Sincero, Jen. *You Are a Badass: How to Stop Doubting Your Greatness and Start Living an Awesome Life.* Running Press, 2017.

Wieder, Marcia. *Dream: Clarify and Create What You Want.* Next Century Publishing, 2016.

MOVIES:

Anything with a strong female lead and a happy ending.

The Devil Wears Prada (2006)
Diary of a Mad Black Women (2005)
Pretty Woman (1990)
Erin Brokovich (2000)
*basically anything Julia Roberts does
Bad Teacher (2011)
The Sweetest Thing (2002)
The Other Woman (2014)

plus a million more....

When I Go Really Old-School with movies:

The Wizard of Oz (1939)
Gone With The Wind (1939)

TED TALKS:

Sarah Knight: The Magic of Not Giving A F*ck (Life changing and funny)
https://www.youtube.com/watch?v=GwRzjFQa_Og&t=29s

James Veitch: This is What Happens When You Reply to Spam Email (not life changing but hilarious)
https://www.youtube.com/watch?v=_QdPW8JrYzQ

There's so much great information out there to help you change your mind and change your life. Explore. Enjoy. Life is good. Like, it really is good.

AUTHOR BIO

Lisa M. Zawistowski

Better known as Lisa Z., Lisa is a happiness and success coach, writer, blogger, and author of the book "Get What You Want. Get Clear, Get Real and Get Going." She is also owner and heart-centered CEO at www.smallsteps2bigchange.com, where you can grab her FREE guides, including Hardwire Yourself to Be Happy: 26 Ways to Hoist Your Happy to New Heights. You can also sign up for her new workshop, Unleash Your Inner Badass and find out how to work one on one with her to change YOUR life.

Lisa is a contributor to Addicted2Success.com, Thrive Global and previously to Huffington Post and Smart Healthy Women magazine. Lisa has studied business and psychology at the undergraduate and graduate levels and has completed strategic intervention plus relationship and divorce prevention coach training with Tony Robbins' Robbins-Madanes Institute. She is a life-long fitness enthusiast, traveler, hugger and animal lover residing with her family in sunny FL, USA. Her motto: Change your mind, change your life. Start today.

Acknowledgements

First and foremost, thank you Alexa for that predestined night in the McDonald's drive-thru more than a decade ago where you were being authentically you and so right about getting what we want. Thank you for being my fabulous daughter and friend. Thank you, Jason, for requesting McDonald's so that Alexa could tell me to get what I want. You are, without a doubt, the kindest soul I've ever known. And, more importantly, thank you both for being amazing humans who have hands down taught me more than I have taught you. You both continue to make my world better than I could ever have imagined.

Thank you to my husband, best friend and life partner for thirty-four years and counting. I am forever grateful for your belief in me and your continued willingness to support my dreams. We have seen good times and bad, richer and poorer, sickness but mostly health thankfully, and ease and challenge. I could not have a better person to go through this thing called life with. And, you are funny. No arguments. You just are.

Thank you to my besties who have been with me for decades and always inspire me to be the best version of myself and love me just the same when I'm not. To Denise, girl, you have stood the test of time with me from the earliest days in the tent promising we'd never date each others' exes and all night reading sleepovers with Harlequin Romances to the challenges of time, money and distance that have tried, sometimes successfully, to keep us apart. But never for long and never mentally or spiritually. To Gretchen, this book literally would not exist without you. You are by far its biggest supporter and my daily cheerleader. For the number of times I "ran" things by you, asked you to read a chapter, laid on my floor depressed and unable to write, struggled with the title and other issues ad nauseum, and so much more, I am literally forever grateful. To Lori, who inspires me in so many ways and makes me laugh. You have the kindest heart, and an infectious childlike enthusiasm and a similar ability to hold your liquor, until we don't, of course. I will always dip my toes in the Pacific with you. Thank you to my Auntie, my absolute life-long personal champion and friend. You have given me a boost more times than I could ever count and reminded me who I am when I have needed it most. Thank you to Lisa York for taking time out of your busy day to listen to audios of the chapter and provide the most thoughtful insights.

Thank you to my many coaches and mentors, to my book coach Alisia Leavitt, my Improv teacher John Huls, my storytelling coach Marianne Hayes, and to my cousin, the astonishingly talented writer, Andrew S. Lewis. All of you have helped me create this book and nurtured me becoming more me.

Thank you to all my clients, those I've interviewed, chatted with and observed online and in person for contributing to this book though you didn't know it.

Thank you to all my family and friends who make my life rich and meaningful each in your own way.

Thank you to my mom because whatever our past and our differences may be, you have contributed much to who I am, and I can only be grateful for that.

www.ingramcontent.com/pod-product-compliance
Lightning Source LLC
Chambersburg PA
CBHW032113090426
42743CB00007B/342